The Blue Heron Ranch Cookbook

Recipes and Stories
from a Zen Retreat Center

Nadia Natali

Illustrated by Marica Natali Thompson

North Atlantic Books
Berkeley, California

Dedication

I dedicate this book to my wonderful husband Enrico, who has been by my side through many lives, and who in this lifetime has been my best friend and partner. I feel very lucky to share his life.

And to my lovely children—Vincenzo, Francesca, and Marica—who bring a beauty and truth into my life that I am most grateful to discover.

Lastly, I dedicate this book most especially to my Andrei, my youngest child, who loved this land more than anyone and who is no longer with us in this beautiful and challenging world.

Contents

Acknowledgments

....

I first and foremost thank my daughter Marica, who illustrated and
helped design this whole project and tested recipes.

I also thank my daughter Francesca and Mary Ann Short,
who edited the manuscript with great enthusiasm.

Most especially I thank Margaret Dodd, whose professionalism
and warmth made the last lap of this journey a delight.

And of course I thank my husband Enrico for the never-ending
help and support he provided throughout.

Preface

Ten miles north of Ojai, at the end of a very long road in Matilija (pronounced Ma-til-i-ha) Canyon, lies Blue Heron Ranch. It nestles within the Los Padres National Forest in southern California. Here we, the Natali family, have faced fires, floods, bears, mountain lions, and rattlesnakes. We built a home, raised a family of three children, and have run a modest Zen center and fed a myriad of visitors for twenty-five years. This cookbook was inspired by the many individuals who visited our center and encouraged me to write about the meals prepared for our retreats.

Interspersed with the recipes, I've included stories about Blue Heron's beginnings and how it has evolved. In addition to the recipes and stories, I've offered tips on cooking for a crowd and fresh ideas that you can use for weekend visits of friends or family members. Or perhaps you're starting your own retreat center! You'll find a good sequence of meals to serve to a small group over a weekend, along with helpful shopping lists.

My daughter Marica has drawn the piquant and charming illustrations, her vision and version of our family and life as she grew up on Blue Heron Ranch.

I cordially invite you to enter our home, by way of this book, and share in our meals and our stories.

Introduction

Located ninety miles north of Los Angeles, Blue Heron Ranch encompasses forty acres of land we purchased twenty-seven years ago. In 1990 we built a zendo on our land and our Zen retreat center was born. It has evolved to include a more East-West flavor by offering other weekend retreats, including trauma-release work and therapy-through-dance workshops. Many people come through our center to attend our workshops and meditations, and we provide all the meals. As ranch cook, I have learned the importance of knowing how to prepare for all contingencies, whether it be an extended-family gathering, a large retreat, or even my own nuclear family when we're rained in. Since we live far from town, it's critical for me to think ahead and be prepared to serve meals with no possibility of resupply for several weeks running.

You too, with minimum effort, can find a comfortable way to prepare meals for a number of people for several days at a time. If you're interested in how I've worked out the preliminary organization for a weekend retreat, I describe it here. If, however, you don't anticipate needing to plan ahead to feed a crowd, jump to the next chapter.

We ask people to bring their own bedding, towels, and flashlight. For formal retreats, we provide a bundle of dishes, silverware, and cloth napkins for each participant, to be used through the whole weekend. Each participant washes his or her own dishes and utensils after meals and returns them to the dining table. For each meal, I assign a different person to help me and give sole responsibility to two other people for cleanup. The helpers rotate until everyone has worked on both kitchen prep and kitchen cleanup. Since I'm cooking all the meals, I make sure the kitchen is in order before we sit down to eat; this makes cleanup easier, especially for those not familiar with the kitchen.

Menus for Family Gatherings and Retreats

Typical Menus

The following is a typical menu for a formal retreat weekend, along with a list of foods and staples from which you can compile your own grocery list.

Friday Dinner

Blue Heron Ranch Potato Leek Soup on page 72
Whole Wheat Bread and butter on page 114
Cool Cucumber Salad on page 98
Cookies on pages 168–170

Saturday Breakfast

Sesshin Oatmeal on page 132

Home-Baked Granola on page 134

Cloved Fruit Compote on page 104

Simply Miso Soup on page 70

Soft-boiled eggs

Toast and jam

Serve with all breakfast recipes:

Milk and soy milk

Maple syrup

Green onions for miso soup

Salt and pepper

Saturday Lunch

Blue Heron Beans on page 31

Seasoned Rice on page 30

Desert Hummus on page 200

Pesto Lemon Sauce on page 197

Baby Green Salad on page 96

Blue Heron Salad Dressing on page 95

I prepare the beans and rice just after breakfast so I'm free for the activities of the morning.

Saturday Afternoon Tea

Cookies, cake, or pie
Milk and soy milk
Honey and/or sugar

An assortment of teas:
herbal
decaffeinated
black

Saturday Dinner

Spaghetti and sauce
Steamed broccoli
Baby Green Salad on page 96
Garlic bread

The sauce can be cooked the
day before and refrigerated.

Sunday Breakfast

Early Morning Rice Cream on page 133
Fruit (bananas or berries)

Same condiments as Saturday
Breakfast with a different
hot cereal and fruit

Sunday Lunch
(chiefly leftovers)

Soup from Friday night
Blue Heron Beans leftovers
Spaghetti and sauce leftovers

Baby Green Salad on page 96
Tea and cookies or cake

Suggestion if more food is needed:
Quiche on pages 48 or 49
Sunday Stuffed Potatoes on page 44

Food and Supply List

You'll want to purchase your food ahead of time. I usually buy staple items like paper napkins sometime during the prior week, and I purchase perishables the morning of the day the retreat starts. I plan ahead for three days at a time unless, of course, we have a flooded-in situation, which most of my readers needn't worry about.

Below I itemize from my personal list, which I refer to as the Template List, all the foods and items you might want to consider stocking up on.

Template List for Six People
for Two Days, Including Six Meals

The following list may look daunting, but it is not as much food as you think. You may have many of these ingredients already. Please bear in mind that the tastiness of your food depends on the quality of the ingredients.

2 qts	Soy milk		1 lb	Goat cheese
1 lb	Butter		1 lb	Yellow miso
1 24-oz jar	Apple sauce		1 8-oz	Maple syrup
2 cups	Rolled oats		1 cup	Rice cream
6 cups	Granola		1 cup	Dried fruit mix
2 lbs	Spaghetti		1 lb	Elbow noodles
2 qts	Chicken or veggie broth		1 jar	Dried red peppers, flakes
1 8-oz	Vinegar		1 jar	Oregano
1 jar	Thyme		1 jar	Dill
1 8-oz	Mirin rice wine		1 bag	Cookies, favorite
2 28-oz	Tomatoes, canned		1 jar	Bay leaf
1 12-oz	Balsamic vinegar		1 16-oz	Extra virgin olive oil
1 lb	Parmesan cheese		4	Avocados
2 cups	Black beans		1 cup	Lima beans
2 cups	Kidney beans		1 cup	Anasazi beans
2 each	Teas: black, herb, decaf		1 lb	Honey, sugar, or stevia

Perishables

These items need to be bought the day they are needed or the evening before:

1 gallon	Milk	2 doz	Eggs
2 loaves	Whole wheat bread	1 doz	Tortillas
1 large loaf	French bread	2 lbs	Firm tofu
2 pints	Hummus	2 pints	Salsa
8	Apples	6	Bananas
6	Baking potatoes	6	New potatoes
1 bunch	Celery	4	Leeks
2 bunches	Green onions	3	Cucumbers
6 heads	Lettuce (or bags of mixed baby greens)	2	Onions
		1 lb	Mushrooms
3 bunches	Broccoli	3	Red peppers

Staples

The following list is mainly to be used for checking to see that you already have enough of these items:

Toilet paper	Tissues	Paper napkins
Matches	Candles	Bottled water
Flashlights	Batteries	First aid kit
Aspirin or Advil	Sanitary supplies	Natural Bug Off
Sunscreen		

Our Arrival

On December 8, 1980, Enrico and I stood together at the brown metal gate where the pavement ends on Matilija Canyon Road. Parked nearby was our old Jeep, which was hauling a modest foldout camper, our new home. It was a beautiful, warm, dry day and we were waiting for a Forest Service employee to bring us the key granting access to our property in the Los Padres National Forest. Our newly purchased land was a mile farther up the canyon, in a remote area with no electrical, gas, or phone lines and no possibility of putting them in. No one lived nearby except the family residing near the gate where we stood waiting that day.

When Dave eventually came, he handed us the key along with some advice on what we should be prepared for. He warned us about the perpetual threat of forest fire, which hadn't occurred in the area for fifty years, and the winter rains, which can swell the two rivers crossing the road to our property into raging torrents. Then, of course, there were rattlesnakes, coyotes, and sometimes mountain lions and bears. But the most dangerous threat, Dave said, were the hikers: "There can be some real kooks out there." We thanked him, not quite sure how to hear all that. We didn't yet understand the implications of the warnings we'd just heard, so we simply took them in, pushed them aside, and concerned ourselves with what was in front of us.

It was time to venture past the gate and find a clearing for the trailer before dark. The chaparral all around was so thick that new growth underneath wasn't even possible; sunlight couldn't penetrate the brush. We had to get down on all fours to see through the thicket. Finally Enrico found a small clearing among the wild cherry and ceanothus just outside our property line. We set up camp, hoping that within a couple of weeks we could clear a little road with space enough at the end for our trailer. Manzanita trees surrounded our campsite. It was unusual to find in one spot so many of these small hardwoods that look like large bonsai trees with smooth, blood-red bark. The air was rich with the scent of yerba santa and sage, and bees and hummingbirds buzzed around our heads. What a fabulous place!

How sharply our new surroundings contrasted with the snow of northern New York, where we had spent the previous eight years. And how funny that we should again find ourselves living at the end of a mile-long dirt road, as we had in the north country.

Our cabin in the woods in Sackets Harbor had been a cozy little place, originally built by Enrico's father. We fixed it up, putting in heat and water, but were away several months each year traveling around the country so Enrico could photograph. On these trips, I read and cooked while Enrico spent each day taking pictures for his project. We would choose roads that were off the main highways and camp along the way. Our trips usually ended in Ojai, California. We timed our arrivals to hear Krishnamurti talk. Krishnamurti was a man of unusual substance and truth, and thousands of eager people wanting to transform their lives came to his talks. After three yearly visits to Ojai, we decided to make it our new home.

Our funds didn't measure up to the prices in town, but a friend led us to a forty-acre parcel out in the middle of the National Forest, ten miles north of town. The land was inexpensive because it wasn't properly surveyed and was off the grid, having no utilities. The fact that it was off the grid and that the river couldn't be crossed for weeks at a time during the rainy season deterred many. Yet we felt we had really lucked out. Little did we know the extent of our naiveté.

Each day I hauled water from the river back to the trailer to wash our dishes and cook our meals. Ice chests and propane tanks created a kitchen that I found easy to work with, having camped out for so many years. Our first-born daughter Francesca was only three-and-a-half. She and I often walked together down to the river through the prickly chaparral, to swim, play, fill our pails, and drink the clear water.

The canyon river that winds through our land is small and inviting, with a perfect swimming hole that we named Ladybug Pool. A huge boulder on one side is big enough to seat many people. Across the water, a long, flat bedrock slants steeply up toward the sun. It spoke to me of intense earthquakes and, one day while relaxing by the water, I realized that the riverbed might be a fault line. I numbly stared at it, not wanting to acknowledge this frightening possibility. But, despite my initial trepidation and despite the 1980s quakes in the Los Angeles area, only ninety miles away, to this day we've never felt more than a minor tremor at Blue Heron Ranch, the name we picked for our property.

Vegetarian Dinners

My Favorite Tomato Sauce

Spaghetti has been one of our family's favorite meals. We have it at least once a week. It's so simple and quick to cook, yet is always delicious. When the children were young they always asked for it. I usually prepare this meal on the second evening of our meditation retreats.

Sauce

1. In a medium pot over medium heat cook onions until translucent, **5 minutes**. Onions taste best when sauted by themselves a few minutes before adding anything else.

2 Tbs	**Olive oil**
2	**Onions** sliced

2. Add:

1 head	**Garlic** diced
1	**Red pepper** sliced
6	**Shiitake mushrooms** sliced

3. **Cook for at least 20 minutes**. It is best cooked down for an hour.

3 28-oz cans	**Whole tomatoes** sliced
¼ cup	**Red wine**
1 Tbs	**Oregano** dried or ¼ cup fresh
	Salt to taste

Spaghetti

4. In a large pot, bring to a boil:

8 cups	**Water**
1 Tbs	**Olive oil**

5. When it starts bubbling add: Cook as directed on package. Rinse immediately.

1 lb	**Angel-hair pasta**

Serve with **¹/2 cup Parmesan cheese** grated

Grandma Elizabeth's Polenta

Polenta, or cornmeal, is a typical meal eaten in Italy. You use a tomato sauce to pour over it, but you don't mix it in. Enrico told me that when he was little his mother would serve polenta on a huge wooden board in the middle of the table. She would pour it out in the exact middle and then the sauce would be poured on top of that. All five children, plus the two parents, would start eating from their edge and make their way towards the middle. It tasted great.

Then one day his mother changed her mind and began serving it on a platter. Enrico said it no longer tasted as good. I loved the idea of the wooden board and we have eaten it that way ourselves. It is great fun for adults as well as children.

1. Prepare **My Favorite Tomato Sauce** *on page 24.*

2. In a medium-size pot combine:

2 cups	**Cornmeal**
1/4 cup	**Parmesan cheese** grated
1/4 tsp	**Salt**

3. Mix in slowly so as to avoid lumping:

2 cups	**Milk**
2 cups	**Water**

4. Cook on low heat for **20 minutes** until thick.

    Serve with **1/2 cup Parmesan cheese** grated

Lasagna from Enrico's Family

Serves 10

Enrico's family came from Morolo, Italy. Both his parents' families came from the same village near Rome; however, his parents met and married in northern New York. Whenever there is a birthday or special occasion I make lasagna. It is rich with cheese, but for such an occasion you want something special. I make two or three for large groups, baking it a day ahead. Refrigerate it after it has cooled. Take it out early the next day so it has time to return to room temperature. To reheat, set the oven at 350° and bake for 20 to 30 minutes, or until piping hot. Let it cool a little before serving.

1. In a medium pot saute:

2 Tbs	**Olive oil**
1	**Onion** sliced
1	**Green bell pepper** sliced
1/2 lb	**Mushrooms** sliced
1 head	**Garlic** sliced

2. Add and let **simmer 20 minutes or more**:

2 28-oz cans	**Tomatoes** crushed
1/4 cup	**Red wine**
1 tsp each	**Dill, oregano, basil**
1/2 cup	**Water**

3. In a separate bowl, mix together and set aside:

1 32-oz	**Ricotta cheese**
2	**Eggs**
1 Tbs	**Rosemary** cut small

4. In another bowl grate:

1 lb	**Mozzarella cheese**

5. You will also need the following for layering, on the next page:

1/2 cup	**Parmesan cheese** grated
1 lb	**Lasagna noodles**

Lasagna Layering

Preheat oven to 350°.

In a large (approximately 10 x 15-inch) glass baking pan, layer as follows:

1. Sauce: A little on bottom of pan to cover surface

2. Noodles: Lay out flat; usually 5 or 6 will fit;
    break off any corners if necessary

3. Ricotta cheese: Spread 1/2 amount over noodles (about 2 cups)

4. Mozzarella cheese: Sprinkle 1/3 amount (1 1/2 cups each layer)

5. Parmesan cheese: Sprinkle 1/3 amount (3 Tbs each layer)

6. Sauce: Spread 1/2 amount (a little less than 2 cups)

7. Repeat steps: 2 through 6

*Sprinkle leftover
Mozzarella and
Parmesan cheeses
on top of everything.*

Bake at 350° for 45 minutes.
Let cool for 15 minutes before serving.

Matilija Manicotti

······························· *Serves 8* ·······························

Matilija, a canyon in Ojai where our home is located, is a rough and rug-
ged place that creates a hearty appetite. My youngest son Andrei loved
manicotti. It is very similar to lasagna, yet Andrei always liked it more
because he could see the long stuffed noodles.

Sauce

1. In a medium pot saute:

2 Tbs	**Olive oil**
8 cloves	**Garlic** minced
1 28-oz can	**Whole tomatoes**
¼ cup	**Wine**
1 Tbs	**Oregano**
1 Tbs	**Basil**

2. Cook in a large pot according to
   directions:
   Cook until al dente, or not too soft.

1½ boxes	**Manicotti noodles** (14 noodles)

Filling

3. Mix in a large bowl:

2 lbs	**Ricotta cheese**
1	**Egg**
¼ cup	**Parmesan cheese**
⅛ tsp	**Nutmeg**
1 tsp	**Dill**
12 oz	**Mozzarella cheese** grated

4. Put a little tomato sauce on the
   bottom of a 9 x 12-inch glass baking dish.

5. Stuff the noodles with filling. (I use
   my fingers to fill the noodles.)

6. Place stuffed noodles in baking dish
   and pour the rest of the sauce over the
   noodles.

Bake at 350° for 35 minutes.

Pizza with Goat Cheese

.... *Makes three 15-inch pizzas* ....

Beware, homemade pizza will spoil you. You will find it hard to buy pizza after baking your own. This is a special delight and well worth the effort for family and friends.

Preheat oven to 425°.

1. Prepare **My Favorite Tomato Sauce** *on page 24.*

Dough

2. Heat in a small pot until just warm:
   A good way to test is to splash a drop
   on your wrist; if it is just warm it is ready.

3 cups	**Milk** or **soy milk**
2 Tbs	**Honey**
1/4 cup	**Olive oil**

3. Remove from heat and add:

2 Tbs	**Dry yeast**
8 cups	**Whole wheat flour**
1 tsp	**Salt**

4. Mix, knead, and let rise in its bowl in a warm place for 1/2 hour.

5. Punch down dough and divide into three balls. With a rolling pin flatten and press out the dough on a floured board, then carefully place rolled-out dough on the oiled pizza pans.

Topping

6. Add 1/3 amount of each of the following to each pizza, in the order listed:

   Bake at 400° for 25 minutes.

3 1/2 cups	**Tomato sauce**
2 lbs	**Mozzarella cheese** grated
2 large	**Bell peppers** sliced
1/2 cup	**Goat cheese** crumbled
1/4 cup	**Parmesan cheese** grated

   Optional toppings:
   Red onions, mushrooms, olives, pepperoni, and others of your choice

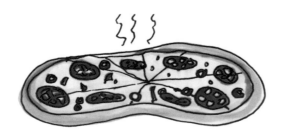

Seasoned Rice

.... *Serves 6* ....

We use rice more than any other grain. It is mild and nonallergenic for the most part, and it can go with almost any meal.

1. In a medium pot, mix together and cover:

4	cups	**Water**
1	Tbs	**Butter**
2	cups	**Brown rice, brown basmati** or **jasmine** rinsed and drained
1	Tbs	**Butter**
1	stick	**Kombu** broken into pieces

2. Bring water to a boil. Reduce heat. **Cook for 45 minutes.** Let sit for 10 minutes.

   For white basmati rice, bring to boil and **cook for 15 minutes.**

3. In a large pan, saute:

1 Tbs	**Butter**
1	**Onion** sliced fine
4	**Shiitake mushrooms** sliced

4. Continue to saute vegetables until soft, then add cooked rice and stir all the ingredients until they are evenly warm.

5. Season to taste with approximately:

2 Tbs	**Tamari** soy sauce

Blue Heron Beans

This delicious but simple meal is one of our favorites. I serve this dish for lunch at my dance workshops and the students always like it. It is easy to prepare the night before and reheat it at mealtime. I always use a pressure cooker but you can soak the beans overnight and cook until tender, around one hour. Older dried beans take more time.

1. While sorting the beans, heat in a large pot:

8 cups	Water

2. Sort through for tiny stones or cracked or bad-colored beans. Rinse in a colander, then add to pot of water:

1 cup	Black beans
1/2 cup	Lima beans
1/2 cup	Kidney beans
1/2 cup	Anasazi or pinto beans

3. Add to pot:

   When cooked, drain beans of most of the liquid.

2 cloves	Garlic
1 tsp	Chili powder
1 tsp	Rosemary
1 tsp	Thyme
3	Bay leaves dried or fresh

4. Important to serve with:

2 cups	Green Enchilada Sauce *on page 196*
2 cups	Desert Hummus *on page 200*
1 cup	Pesto
2 cups	Guacamole

5. About an hour before beans are finished cooking, start cooking brown rice:

3 cups	Jasmine brown rice uncooked
6 cups	Water or according to directions

Serve with:
Baby Green Salad *on page 96*
Goat Cheese Salad *on page 103*

Adzuki Beans and Rice

.... *Serves 6* ....

This Japanese bean and rice combination is both very tasty and healthy.
Too bad more people don't know how good this easy and unusual recipe is.

1. In a medium pot combine:

1	cup	**Adzuki beans** rinsed and picked over
1	cup	**Brown rice** rinsed
5	cups	**Water**
1		**Onion** chopped small
2	Tbs	**Tamari** soy sauce

2. Heat until water boils, then
   reduce heat to low setting.

   Cook for 1¹/2 hours.

   Serve with:
   Baby Green Salad *on page 96*
   Goat Cheese Salad *on page 103*

Black Bean Enchiladas

Marica's husband, Justin, loves enchiladas, particularly with green sauce. Enchiladas can be cooked with just about anything inside, so let yourself be creative.

1. In a shallow bowl:

2. Pour half of chili sauce on the bottom of a large 9 x 12-inch baking dish.

3. Dip both sides into remaining sauce until tortillas are mostly covered:

4. Prepare and fill each tortilla with 1/4 cup:

5. Sprinkle 2 Tbs of cheese over beans in each tortilla.

6. Pour 1 heaping Tbs of tomato in each tortilla:

4 cups	**Green Enchilada Sauce** *on page 196 or you can buy it prepared in a health food store*
12	**Flour tortillas** or **18 corn tortillas**
5 cups	**Black beans** cooked
6 oz	**Jack cheese**
8 oz	**Mozzarella cheese** grated
1/2 cup	**Tomatoes** diced or **tomato sauce**

7. Roll up the tortillas and place in long baking dish side by side.

8. Pour the rest of the **Green Enchilada Sauce** across the rolled tortillas.

9. Add the rest of the cheese across the top of the tortillas.

   Bake at 350° for 15–20 minutes or until cheese is melted.

   Options: Fill with cooked **chicken** or **rice**

Ojai Chili

This is a winner, and as you can see, you just throw everything in, and it works. It is a great dish on a cold wintry day or evening.

1. In a large pot of boiling water reduce heat, **cook 1 or 1½ hours,** until just soft:

1½ cups	**Kidney beans** picked over and rinsed

2. In a large pot, saute:

2 Tbs	**Olive oil**
2	**Onions**
1 head	**Garlic** sliced

3. Add to the beans:

2 28-oz cans	**Whole tomatoes** sliced
½ cup	**Red wine**
¼ cup	**Lemon juice**
1 pkg	**Corn** frozen
1 pkg	**Lima beans** frozen
1 pkg	**Peas** frozen
2 Tbs	**Mustard** Dijon
1 Tbs each	**Dill, oregano, basil chili powder, cumin**

4. Cook until hot.

5. Add, stir in, and cook for no more than a couple of minutes:

1 lb	**Tofu** cubed

Serve with:
Brown Rice
Baby Green Salad *on page 96*

Sauteed Vegetables with Rice

Serves 6

This is a most ordinary dish yet it never loses its appeal. You can use almost any vegetable you like or that is available; you will never tire of it.

Cut all vegetables in large bite-size pieces

1. In a large skillet, saute until translucent:	**2 Tbs**	**Olive oil**
	2	**Onions**
2. Add and cook:	**1 head**	**Broccoli** cut into medium-bite sizes
3. Add:	**2**	**Red bell peppers** cubed, large bite-size
	1/2 lb	**Mushrooms** preferably Portabella
	1 Tbs	**Ginger** peeled and chopped small
	1 head	**Garlic** chopped small
	2	**Zucchini** medium-size, sliced thin
4. Add, near the end of cooking:	**1 lb**	**Tofu** cut into cubes
5. Season with:	**2 Tbs**	**Tamari** soy sauce
	1 tsp	**Dill**
	1 tsp	**Turmeric**
	1 tsp	**Thyme**

Serve over:
Brown rice or **rice noodles** with
a few drops of *Hot Pepper Sesame Oil*
made by Eden

Special Vegetables with Almonds

.... *Serves 4* ....

This stir-fry dish is made special with some new ideas.

1. In a large skillet saute ingredients, adding in the order given:

   Let each vegetable cook a little before adding the next one.

2 Tbs	**Olive oil**
2	**Onions** chopped in large pieces
2 heads	**Broccoli** cut into small pieces
2	**Shiitake mushrooms** cut into bite-size pieces
1½ cups	**Edamame** soy beans without the pods
1 bunch	**Swiss chard** remove stalk
1 lb	**Tofu** or **tempeh** cubed

2. In a small metal pan, toast until just browned:

   1 cup   **Almonds** cracked*

   Serve over:
   Brown rice or **rice noodles** with a few drops of *Hot Pepper Sesame Oil* made by Eden

*To crack almonds:
Place them in the middle of a folded kitchen towel, then crack them with a hammer on a rug on the floor.

Vincenzo's Risotto

······················· *Serves 6* ·······················

Vincenzo is my wonderful stepson, whom I've had the luck to know since he was three years old. Lately, he has been busy making movies but still visits often. When he's here he sometimes makes his delicious risotto.

1. In a medium pot saute:

2 Tbs	**Olive oil**
1	**Onion** sliced thin

2. After 5 minutes, add:

2 cups	**Arborio rice** rinsed and drained
1 Tbs	**Butter**
8 cups	**Soup stock** vegetable or chicken

3. Stir for another 5 minutes, then add:

1 cup	**White wine**

4. Bring to boil.
    Cook uncovered for 15 minutes.

5. Add:

1 cup	**Parmesan cheese** grated

    Cover and let sit for 10 minutes.

Serve with:
Miso Pine Salmon *on page 54*
Baby Green Salad *on page 96*

Carrots and Tofu

.... *Serves 6* ....

This combination of vegetables and tofu is exceptional, especially with the Matilija Tamari Sauce on page 194. This dish gets more tasty if you marinate it in the sauce a few hours and reheat.

1. In a medium-size pot add enough water to cover steamer (1¼ inches). Steam until soft:

1 lb	**Baby carrots** whole

2. In a large skillet saute over medium heat:

2 Tbs	**Olive oil**
2	**Onions** sliced into large pieces
2	**Red bell peppers** sliced into large pieces
1 head	**Garlic** cut into large pieces

3. Cook for **5 minutes** or so. Then add cooked carrots to sauteed mixture.

4. Add:

1 lb	**Tofu** cut into bite-size pieces

5. Add the **Matilija Tamari Sauce** *on page 194.*

Serve over any rice recipe.

Lentils and Mint

Mint adds a nice variation to lentil recipes.

1. In a medium pot saute:

| 2 Tbs | Olive oil |
| 1 head | Garlic minced |

2. Add, bring to a boil and lower heat:

8 cups	Water
2 cups	French green lentils* rinsed and drained
1 cup	Apple juice unfiltered
2 Tbs	Ginger fresh and minced
1/2 cup	Mint leaves fresh and chopped

Cook for 20 minutes.

French green lentils are not easy to find but are preferable with this recipe.

Serve with:

Desert Hummus Sauce *on page 200*

Curried Lentils

Here is another wonderful lentil dish.

1. In a large pot saute dry:	**1 Tbs**	**Mustard seed** until gray
2. Add and cook **about 5 minutes**:	**2 Tbs**	**Olive oil**
	2	**Onions** sliced thin
3. Add:	**3 cups**	**Water**
	1¹/₂ cups	**Red lentils** rinsed and drained
	¹/₂ cup	**Cranberries** dried, or **raisins**
	3 cups	**Carrots** 6–8 sliced bite-size
	2 Tbs	**Butter**
	³/₄ tsp	**Curry powder**
	¹/₂ cup	**Green fennel leaves** fresh or **1 tsp ground dried fennel**
		Salt to taste
		Black pepper to taste

Cook ¹/₂ hour.

Serve with:
Raita Salad *on page 106*

California Split Pea Dahl

A wonderful California version of traditional Indian dahl.

1. In a dry, medium pot heat only a few minutes until gray: *Be careful not to burn.*	**1 Tbs**	**Mustard seeds**
2. Add:	**2 Tbs** **1**	**Olive oil** **Onion** sliced
3. Add and simmer covered for 1½ hours**.**	**5½ cups** **2 cups** **1 tsp** **½ tsp** **1 tsp**	**Water** or **soup stock** **Split peas** rinsed **Turmeric** **Curry powder** **Lemon juice**
4. Spoon 2 Tbs on top of each serving:	**1 pint**	**Yogurt** or **sour cream**

Serve with:
Pucci's Potato and Egg Curry *on page 43*
Spinach and Anaheim Chilies *on page 46*

Pucci's Potato and Egg Curry

.... *Serves 6* ....

Pucci, who is originally from India, and her two daughters, Priya and Kavitha, used to visit here all the time. The girls were and still are very good friends with Francesca and Marica and became a close part of our family. Pucci would often make us an Indian dinner, which was a great treat. This egg curry dish is my interpretation of what I remember her cooking.

1. In a small pot, cook for 10 minutes in boiling water:

   6 — **Eggs** cooled and peeled

2. Steam separately in medium pot:
   Cook until just soft, using a fork to test.

   8 — **New potatoes**

3. In a large skillet saute until translucent:

   2 Tbs **Olive oil**
   2 **Onions**
   1 pinch **Salt**

4. Add hardboiled eggs and potatoes sliced.

5. Mix in gently:

   1/2 tsp **Turmeric powder**
   1/4 Tbs **Chili powder**
   1 tsp **Curry powder**
   1 **Carrot** grated

Serve with
California Split Pea Dahl *on page 42*

Sunday Stuffed Potatoes

························· *Serves 6* ·······························

These potatoes are so easy and so much more tasty than plain baked potatoes. My kids love them and so do the others who come through during our retreats. We usually serve them on Sundays.

Preheat oven to 425°.

1. Wash and pierce a couple of times with a fork:

2. Place potatoes on a buttered cookie sheet or in a large baking dish.

   Bake at 425° for 45 minutes until a fork pierces them easily.

3. Remove the potatoes from oven and cut them in half lengthwise. Let cool until you can handle them.

4. Scoop the inside of the potatoes out into a large bowl, taking care to keep the skin intact for stuffing later.

5. Add to bowl and mix together:

6. Gently pack the mixture into the potato skins. Sprinkle on top:

7. Return to oven and **bake at 350° for 20 minutes** or until warm again.

6	**Baking potatoes** best are yellow Yukon Gold

2 Tbs	**Butter**
1/2 cup	**Yogurt**
1/2 cup	**Milk** or **soy milk**
1 cup	**Cheddar cheese** grated
1 tsp	**Dill**
1/4 tsp	**Garlic powder**
	Salt and **black pepper** to taste
	Paprika

Spinach and Anaheim Chilies

Serves 4–6

My friend Pucci inspired me to make this recipe, and I think it is wonderful. Try it—you will agree.

1. In a large skillet saute:

2 Tbs	**Olive oil**
2	**Onions** sliced thin
8	**Anaheim chilies** sliced lengthwise

2. Add and cover pan:

2 bags	**Spinach**
	Salt to taste

   Cook until just soft.

Serve with:
Pucci's Potato and Egg Curry *on page 43*
Basmati Rice

Baked Eggplant

My mother used to make this recipe when I was a child. It is one of my favorite dishes as an adult. I suggest you give it a try.

Preheat oven to 350°.

1. In a large skillet, saute until translucent:

2	Tbs	**Butter**
2		**Onions** sliced
1	head	**Garlic** minced

2. Add to skillet and cook until very soft:

2		**Eggplants** peeled and cubed into small pieces

3. In a separate large bowl, mix together:

4		**Eggs**
2	Tbs	**Tamari**
1	pinch	**Nutmeg**
¼	cup	**Parmesan cheese**
		Salt and **pepper** to taste

4. Place eggplant and onions in a buttered 9 x 9-inch casserole dish.

5. Pour egg mixture over eggplant.

6. Sprinkle on top:

1	cup	**Dry bread crumbs**
2	Tbs	**Parsley** or **cilantro**
2	Tbs	**Parmesan cheese**

Bake at 350° for 20 minutes.

Serve with
Spinach and Anaheim Chilies *on page 46*

Saturday Market Quiche

Serves 6–8

Marica loves to make quiche. Many times she has cooked for our meditation retreats and quiche is her favorite to serve for Sunday lunch.

Preheat oven to 350°.

Buy or make:
Bake crusts in oven for 10 minutes.

2		**Pie crusts** *on page 152*

Quiche Filling

1. In a medium-size covered pot, steam lightly in 1/2 inch water until spinach wilts (5 minutes), then squeeze out excess water and set aside:

1	lb	**Fresh spinach** diced or 1 bag frozen

2. In a large bowl combine:

6		**Eggs**
2	Tbs	**Butter** melted
2½	cups	**Milk** or **soy milk**
2	cups	**Swiss cheese** grated
2	Tbs	**Parmesan cheese**
1	Tbs	**Lemon zest**
1	tsp	**Dill**
1/8	tsp	**Nutmeg**
1/8	tsp	**Salt**
		Black pepper to taste

3. Add vegetables to egg mixture and stir.

4. Pour half of ingredients into each crust.

Bake at 350° for 35 minutes or until firm. Test by shaking it a little. The center may jiggle slightly but should not be sloppy.

Garden Vegetable Quiche

Marica says, "The funny thing about quiche is that you can put just about anything together and it will still come out as a fancy impressive masterpiece. I think the best way to make quiche is to go to a farmer's market and see what catches your eye. Chop it up, put it together, and don't worry too much because you can't go too wrong."

Preheat oven to 350°.

Buy or make:
Bake crusts in oven for 10 minutes.

2	**Pie crusts** *on page 152*

Quiche Filling

1. In a medium skillet, lightly saute:

1 Tbs	**Olive oil**
1/2	**Onion** diced
2	**Zucchinis** diced
2	**Red bell peppers** sliced
1	**Portabella mushroom** sliced

2. In a large bowl combine:

6	**Eggs**
4 Tbs	**Butter** melted
1 1/2 cups	**Milk** or **soy milk**
1 cup	**Cheddar cheese** grated
1 cup	**Jack cheese** grated
2 Tbs	**Parmesan cheese**
1 Tbs	**Lemon zest**
1/8 tsp	**Salt**
1 tsp	**Dill**
	Black pepper to taste

3. Add vegetables to egg mixture and stir.

4. Pour half of ingredients into each crust.

Bake at 350° for 35 minutes or until firm. Test by shaking it a little. The center may jiggle slightly but should not be sloppy.

Fish and Chicken Dinners

Our close friend Kobun Chino Roshi and his family were like members of our own family. They would come and visit us often, and Kobun helped establish our Zen center. He shared many things with us—calligraphy, archery, and cooking. I learned how to cook his delicious meals, and there are three in this book.

Kobun and his youngest daughter Maya are no longer with us on this earthly plane due to a double drowning tragedy in 2002. Our family feels the depth and breadth of the loss and we still hold a big place for them in our hearts.

Kobun's Rice Balls

Kobun showed us this traditional Japanese dish, often prepared ahead for travelling.

1. In a medium pot bring to a boil:

   4 cups Water

2. Add and bring to a boil again, then reduce heat and **cook for 18 minutes**:

   2 cups Japanese rice or **basmati rice**
   rinsed and drained

3. When rice is finished cooking, stir and let it cool and add:

   ⅓ cup Mirin* rice wine
   2 Tbs Rice vinegar*

4. In separate bowls prepare:

   1   Cucumber cut into chunks
   2   Carrots cut into short toothpick slices
   1   Avocado cut into slices
   1 can Albacore tuna drained

5. Fill a small bowl with water and salt. Dip your hands every time before each ball. Roll the rice into balls about 2 inches in diameter. Make a well in the rice then fill with vegetables or fish. Put a scoop of rice on top. Squeeze into a ball, adding rice to edges if necessary. Keep wetting hands in water to rinse them as you work.

6. Cut into narrow strips and crisscross around each rice ball:
   Use a little water as a glue to help the Nori stick. These can be refrigerated up to one day, until you are ready to eat them.

   1 sheet Nori* seaweed

*These ingredients are usually available at health food stores.

Miso Pine Salmon

Serves 6

This recipe was given to me by Kobun Chino Roshi, a Zen teacher and our friend. It is the best salmon I've ever tasted. It is so easy, I use this recipe all the time.

1. Place in a large baking dish:

   2½ lbs   **Fresh salmon** rinsed: score fish crosswise ½-inch deep

2. Mix and spread over entire fish then turn fish skin side up:

   2 Tbs   **Miso paste** mellow white
   2 Tbs   **Water**

4. Find and cut fresh from a tree:

   2 3-inch   **Pine tree branches with needles*** if you can find them

Bake at 500° for 15–20 minutes.
Remove branches before serving.

**Due to fire hazard, do not leave oven unattended.*

**This is optional but will add the special flavor that completes this recipe. Place on top of fish while baking. The branches will turn black.*

Escolar

This fish has a very delicate and rich taste. It can also be expensive but try it for some special occasion. It has recently become endangered, but I couldn't bear to leave this recipe out. You can substitute monkfish or red snapper.

Preheat oven to 375°.

1. Place in a large buttered baking dish:

2 lbs	**Escolar** rinsed

2. In a small pan, heat all together and pour over the fish:

¹/₂ cup	**Butter** melted (1 stick)
1 Tbs	**Lemon juice**
2 cloves	**Garlic** crushed
2 Tbs	**Soy sauce**
¹/₄ cup	**White wine**

Bake at 375° for 15 minutes or until done.

Millennium Paella

This is a very elaborate fish dish that deserves a very special occasion, but it is well worth your while. We have cooked this for New Year's Eve, and it has been a great success. For a larger group of twenty-four, triple the fish and double the amount of rice.

1. Saute, stirring often in a very large pot for **10 minutes**:

2 Tbs	**Olive oil**
2	**Onions** sliced
1 head	**Garlic** diced

2. Add after **5 minutes**:

2	**Red bell peppers** sliced
8	**Whole tomatoes** sliced or canned
1 tsp	**Fennel** ground or fresh

3. Then add when tomatoes are soft:

3 cups	**Arborio rice** first rinsed in cold water
1 pinch	**Saffron**
4 cups	**Chicken stock**
1 cup	**White wine**
1 cup	**Water**

4. In a large pan saute for only **3–4 minutes** stirring constantly:
When cooked, add all to large pot of rice.

18	**Shrimp** cleaned
6 large	**Scallops** cut into quarters
1 lb	**Calamari** sliced into rings

5. Meanwhile, scrub then steam in a large pot (with 2 inches of water) for **5 minutes**:
Keep mussel water for broth. Remove and add to rice pot.

8	**Mussels*** scrape off hairy parts with knife
12	**Clams***

*Very Important: Remove clams or mussels that are tightly closed shut after cooking. This indicates they were dead before cooking and are inedible and harmful.

6. Add monkfish to mussel water and **cook for another 5 minutes.**
Retain broth from mussels.

1 lb	**Monkfish** or any white fish cut into large bite-size pieces

7. Add to rice:
Bake uncovered in large pot, at 225° for 1 hour.

1 cup	**Fish broth** from mussel water

Chicken with Chard and Noodles

Serves 4

This simple and very tasty meal is quick to make.

1. In a large skillet saute about **5 minutes**:

¼ cup	**Sun-dried tomatoes** in oil
2 Tbs	**Olive oil** or oil from dried tomatoes
2	**Onions** sliced

2. Add, cover, and cook on low heat for about **15 minutes**, stirring occasionally until tender and remove from heat:

1 lb	**Chicken breast** cut in long strips
1 bunch	**Swiss chard** rinse and cut off stalks

3. In medium pot bring 8 cups of water to a boil and add:

½ lb	**Rice noodles** (Thai noodles)

   Immediately reduce heat and cook as directed on package.

4. Rinse the noodles, add to the chicken dish, stir, and serve hot.

Francis's Chicken and Curry

Enrico's brother Francis visits us each winter and often cooks for us. This is his delicious recipe.

1. In a large skillet saute:

2 Tbs	**Olive oil**
1	**Onion** sliced

2. Add:

2 tsp	**Curry powder**
4	**Plum tomatoes** canned whole
1/2 cup	**Chicken broth**

3. Add:

1 1/2 lbs	**Chicken breast** rinsed and cut into strips

Simmer for 10 minutes
or until chicken is cooked.

Westport Pineapple Chicken

···················· *Serves 6* ····················

This recipe was my mother's favorite. We lived in Westport, Connecticut, and my mom loved to give large dinner parties several times a year. Her food was always exceptional. I remember, when I was very young, being asked to serve hors d'oeuvres. I took my job very seriously and I felt very important. When the guests sat down to the main course, I was sent to bed, but I always crept down the stairs to watch the festivities through the banister.

Preheat oven to 350°.

1. Place in a large baking dish:

2. Mix together and pour over chicken:

Bake covered at 450° for 45 minutes.
Baste every 15 minutes until done.

3. Add over chicken:

**Bake at 350° uncovered
for 15 minutes more.**

8 small	**Chicken legs and thighs**
1 can	**Frozen orange juice** thawed and undiluted
1 tsp	**Curry powder** mix in with the juice
1/2 cup	**Dried cranberries**
1/2 cup	**Canned mandarin oranges**
1/2 cup	**Canned pineapple** cut into bite sizes
1 cup	**Almonds** cracked*

*To crack almonds:
Place them in the middle of a folded kitchen towel, then crack them with a hammer on a rug on the floor.

Apple-Baked Chicken

.... *Serves 8* ....

Sometimes the simplest things are the best. This may be one of them.

Preheat oven to 350°.

1. Place in large baking pan:

2. Mix and pour over chicken:

3. Sprinkle generously on top of chicken:

1	**Whole chicken** cut into pieces
2 cups	**Apple juice**
½ cup	**Lemon juice** fresh
3 Tbs	**Rosemary** use fresh if possible
3 Tbs	**Whole thyme** use fresh if possible
	Salt and **Pepper** to taste

Bake at 350° for 40 minutes. Turn over and bake **another 15 minutes.**

November Stuffing

Serves 8

For years we were primarily vegetarians and we used to have stuffing at Thanksgiving without the turkey. It seemed quite enough served with all the other typical goodies mentioned below. This recipe can be used alone or as stuffing for a turkey.

1. In a large skillet saute:

2 Tbs	**Olive oil**
2	**Onions** sliced thin
4	**Celery stalks** chopped
1 lb	**Mushrooms** chopped (portabella is wonderful)
1 head	**Garlic** chopped

2. When cooked add:

4	**Apples** cubed into big pieces
1 cup	**Water chestnuts** sliced

3. In a very large bowl add, in the order given, and stir:

2 cups	**Cooked brown rice** precooked the night before or while you are preparing the vegetables
2 boxes	**Stuffing** cubed
7 cups	**Soup stock** chicken or vegetable
1 Tbs	**Curry powder** added to soup stock
1 cup	**Wine**
1/2 cup	**Butter** melted
2 Tbs	**Tamari** soy sauce

4. Gently mix sauteed vegetables into the stuffing mixture.

5. Place loosely in a buttered casserole dish and cover with foil.
   Bake covered at 350° for 45 minutes.
   Bake uncovered for an additional **5 minutes.**

Suggestions for a full holiday dinner would include these side dishes:
Festive Cranberry Sauce *on page 202*
Cooked butternut squash
Cooked broccoli
Apple sauce
Baby Green Salad *on page 96*
Autumn Pumpkin Pie *on page 159*

The Floods

El Niño is a weather condition that can drop eighty inches or more of rain in our canyon in one winter. The first two years we lived here we were spared flood conditions. However, by our third winter we learned how unprepared we were. The rains came unceasingly, and the rivers ballooned. We were able to drive our vehicles in and out until one day, when heading home, we found the rivers raging. Boulders as big as washing machines bobbed down the wild brown river. We couldn't get home. We returned to town and found a gloomy basement apartment to rent from some friends for three months.

That year the rains were so bad that even the road into the canyon was washed out. After many weeks the rivers subsided and Enrico hiked the five miles to our property, walking the torn roads and ripped river bottoms. After he spent weeks clearing flood debris from the road, we joined him, thrilled to be home.

We had traded our foldout trailer for a twenty-two-foot canvas teepee and lived in it for two years while we built our house. By then Francesca was five-and-a-half, our second daughter Marica was two, and I was pregnant! Even in that condition and with our primitive lifestyle, we knew we never wanted to find ourselves barred by Mother Nature from our home again. We soon learned to gauge the conditions. We learned that after accumulating around thirty inches of rainfall in a season, the ground is saturated, and any additional accumulation could cause the rivers to blow out.

When we know a storm is coming we go to town for necessary supplies. We then carefully watch the rain gauge and check the rivers. If we notice the rivers are rising quickly, it is time to take our trucks across the rivers and leave one or two in a safe place on the other side. We drive one truck back, usually our heaviest, and wait. This way we have a vehicle on both sides, so when we can cross the rivers on foot we can drive to town.

We can expect to wait a week or two after a storm before the rivers are calm enough to cross on foot. This is a real art. Accurately judging the height of the water is critical to safely crossing the rapid currents. Our rule of thumb is that the water can be no higher than your crotch. The current is very swift and if it is any higher, you can easily get swept down. One time when Francesca was little, she slipped out of Enrico's hand. Luckily she managed to seize a protruding rock, and Enrico was able to grab her in time.

We eventually found a way to put up a long rope across the rivers during rainy season. Wearing rubber-soled sandals such as Tevas or wetsuit booties is important. They stay on well and you can get a footing without hurting your feet on the rough river bottoms. We wear little or no clothing on our legs so there is less drag, and for the upper body, warm clothing with a short waist. We always carry backpacks with a set of dry clothes inside a plastic bag and change out of our wet things at the truck. When we return, we put our icky wet garments back on, strap on our backpacks filled with food and supplies, and recross the rivers on foot.

Each year I am newly impressed to find the water doesn't feel cold during these conditions. I don't understand why. When there is no more sign of rain and the rivers are low enough, Enrico goes down and moves boulders with the backhoe. Every year the riverbeds change their shape, even in mild winters.

Soups and Stews

Simply Miso Soup

Miso soup is such a delicate and simple delight to drink. We serve it at our weekend retreats for breakfast each morning.

1. In a medium pot bring to a boil:

8 cups	**Water**

2. Turn off heat and add:

1 stalk	**Kombu seaweed** broken into pieces
8 oz	**White miso**
1 tsp	**Honey**
1 Tbs	**Mirin** rice wine
1 tsp	**Rice vinegar**
1/2 tsp	**Handashi*** granular fish, optional
1/2 lb	**Tofu** silken soft, cut into small cubes

3. Just before serving, reheat soup. Do not allow it to boil. Remove from heat.

4. Garnish with or serve in a separate bowl:

3	**Green onions** finely chopped

* This is optional but it is what the restaurants use. You can buy it in bulk at a Japanese store. It has a long shelf life, and gives the soup a different and yummy flavor.

Rainy Day Tofu Soup

·················· *Serves 6* ··················

Another simple and great soup. You can add any vegetable you wish.

1. In a large pot saute:

2 Tbs	**Olive oil**
2	**Onions sliced** cooked until soft

2. Add and bring to a boil, reduce heat:
   Cook 10 minutes.

8 cups	**Vegetable stock**
2	**Carrot** sliced
1 head	**Broccoli** in small peices
8	**Shiitake mushrooms** sliced
4 Tbs	**Mirin** rice wine
1 Tbs	**Tamari** soy sauce
1 stalk	**Kombu seaweed**

3. Add:

8 oz	**Rice noodles**
1 lb	**Tofu**

4. **Cook 2 more minutes** before serving.

   Serve immediately.

Blue Heron Ranch Potato Leek Soup

Serves 8

I usually cook this soup for Friday night dinners when our retreats commence. Soup has a warm welcoming effect, and in the case of a meditation retreat you don't want to start out with too heavy a meal.

1. Saute:

2 Tbs	**Olive oil**
3	**Leeks** cut in thin slices
3 stalks	**Celery** cut in thin slices
1 head	**Garlic** cut in large chunks

2. Add and **cook for 20 minutes**:

8 cups	**Water** or **vegetable** or **chicken stock**
1 Tbs	**Tamari** soy sauce
8	**New potatoes** cubed

3. Add:

¼ lb	**Noodles** elbows style
2 tsp	**Dill**

4. Add when noodles are just done:

1 lb	**Tofu** cubed

Cross-Country Lentil Soup

Serves 8

This soup was inspired by Mark Sandrof, a good friend who many years ago traveled with Enrico and me on a photography trip. We camped every night and cooked our meals on a little Coleman stove, and we ate like royalty.

1. In a large pot saute:

2 Tbs	**Olive oil**
2 large	**Onions** sliced
1 stalk	**Celery** sliced

2. Add:

2	**Carrots** sliced
3	**Potatoes** cubed
1 28-oz can	**Whole tomatoes** sliced
2$^{1}/_{2}$ cups	**Lentils** washed and drained
10 cups	**Water**
$^{1}/_{4}$ cup	**White wine**
2 Tbs	**Lemon juice**
1 Tbs	**Vinegar**
3 Tbs	**Molasses** or honey
2 Tbs	**Tamari** soy sauce
	Salt and **pepper** to taste

Simmer for 1 hour.

Serve with:
Parmesan cheese sprinkled on top
Yogurt a dollop on top

Garbanzo Soup with Tomato

Serves 6

This is so simple and surprisingly tasty. Marica,
in particular, loves this soup.

1. Saute:

2 Tbs	**Olive oil**
2 large	**Onions**

2. Add:

8 large	**New potatoes** cut into cubes
6 fresh	**Tomatoes** or **28-oz can whole tomatoes**
6 cups	**Water**
2 cups	**Garbanzo beans** precooked
1 Tbs	**Curry powder**
2	**Bay leaves**

3. Bring to a boil.
   Simmer for 30 minutes
   or until garbanzo beans are soft.

Winter Minestrone

This soup is great during cold weather.

1. In a large pot bring to a boil and **simmer for 90 minutes:**

8 cups	**Water**
2 cups	**Red kidney beans**
	soak beans overnight to reduce cooking time to 1 hour

2. In a large pot saute:

2 Tbs	**Olive oil**
2 large	**Onions** sliced
1 head	**Garlic** chopped
4 stalks	**Celery** sliced

3. Add:

12 cups	**Water**
6 large	**Carrots** sliced
1 28-oz can	**Tomatoes** whole
1 Tbs	**Lemon juice**
1/2 cup	**Red wine**
1 tsp	**Rosemary**
1 tsp	**Oregano**
1 tsp	**Thyme**
	Salt and **pepper** to taste

4. **Cook 1 1/2 hours.**

5. Add and stir 10 minutes before end of cooking time:

1/2 lb	**Pasta elbows** or **curls**

Serve with **Parmesan cheese**

Southwest Chicken Stew

This delicious soup was cooked and offered to us by Enrico's brother Francis who visits us each winter and in his spare time teaches us to dance the Argentine Tango.

1. **Steam for 15 minutes.** Set aside.

2	**Yams** cubed

2. In a large separate pot cook:

2 Tbs	**Olive oil**
2 Tbs	**Sun-dried tomatoes**
1 lb	**Chicken breast** without skin and cut into slices

3. When chicken is done (**15 minutes**) add to pot and saute:

2 large	**Onions** cut in half and sliced
2 large	**Portabella mushrooms**

4. At this point remove chicken and shred with a fork. Return the chicken to pot.

5. Add and cook:

4 cups	**Chicken broth**
1 28-oz can	**Tomatoes** crushed
1 pkg	**Frozen corn**
1 head	**Broccoli** cut into bite sizes
2 tsp	**Cumin**
1/4 tsp	**Cayenne pepper**

6. Add yams to stew.

Serve with **Parmesan cheese**

San Francisco Chicken Stew

Serves 6

I dreamed of this soup when I was visiting San Francisco, and how it would taste, and even all the ingredients that I would need. When I awoke I gathered together everything that was needed and tried out the recipe. I have made it many times since. It just goes to prove that dreams do come true.

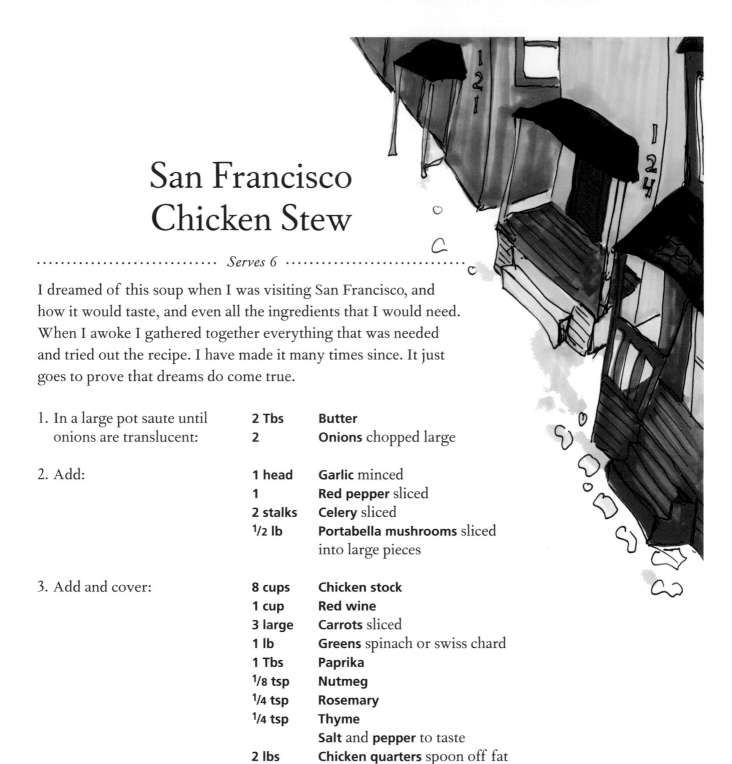

1. In a large pot saute until onions are translucent:

2 Tbs	**Butter**
2	**Onions** chopped large

2. Add:

1 head	**Garlic** minced
1	**Red pepper** sliced
2 stalks	**Celery** sliced
1/2 lb	**Portabella mushrooms** sliced into large pieces

3. Add and cover:

8 cups	**Chicken stock**
1 cup	**Red wine**
3 large	**Carrots** sliced
1 lb	**Greens** spinach or swiss chard
1 Tbs	**Paprika**
1/8 tsp	**Nutmeg**
1/4 tsp	**Rosemary**
1/4 tsp	**Thyme**
	Salt and **pepper** to taste
2 lbs	**Chicken quarters** spoon off fat that floats to the top

Simmer for 1 hour.

Blue Heron Chicken Stew

Serves 6

This stew is great on a cold winter evening.

1. In a large pot saute:

2 Tbs	**Butter**
2	**Onions** cooked until translucent
1 head	**Garlic** minced
1/2 lb	**Mushrooms** sliced in large pieces

2. Add:

8 cups	**Chicken stock**
4 cups	**Water**
1 cup	**White wine**
3 large	**Carrots** sliced into generous bite-size chunks
4	**New potatoes** cubed into large bite-size chunks
1 pint	**Brussels sprouts** if large, cut in half
1 bunch	**Broccoli** cut in small flowerets
2 tsp	**Curry powder**
1/2 tsp	**Salt**
1 lb	**Chicken breast** sliced in long thin pieces
8-oz bag	**Greens** spinach or Swiss chard
1 tsp	**Thyme**

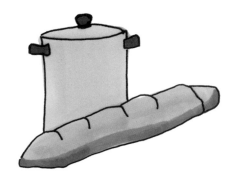

Bring to boil then turn down heat and **simmer for 30 minutes.**

Rainy Day Chicken Noodle Soup

·· *Serves 6* ··

This soup is a variation of Rainy Day Tofu Soup on page 71.

1. In a large pot saute until translucent:

2 Tbs	**Olive oil**
2	**Onions** sliced

2. Cook until soft, then add:

8 cups	**Chicken** or **vegetable stock**
4	**Carrots** sliced
4	**New potatoes** cubed
2	**Portabella mushrooms** sliced
1 large	**Broccoli** cut into bite-size
4 Tbs	**Mirin** rice wine
1 Tbs	**Tamari** soy sauce
1 stalk	**Kombu seaweed**

3. Add:

1 lb	**Chicken breast** sliced

4. **Cook for 25 minutes.**

5. Add and **cook 5 more minutes:**

8 oz	**Rice noodles**

Ojai Bouillabaisse

Ojai has weather similar to the south of France. This stew is very much at home here. I prefer to make it a little more on the delicate side. See what you think.

1. In a large pot saute until onions are translucent:	2 Tbs	**Olive oil**
	4	**Leeks** sliced
	2	**Onions** large slices
	1 head	**Garlic** minced rather large
2. Add and let simmer:	8 cups	**Fish stock** or **chicken stock**
	2 cups	**White wine**
	4 large	**Tomatoes** fresh or canned (whole)
	1/3 cup	**Lemon** juiced
	4	**Carrots** sliced thin
	12	**New potatoes** cut into chunks
	1	**Orange rind** grated
	2 tsp	**Thyme**
	2 tsp	**Marjoram**
3. **Simmer for 15 minutes.**	4	**Bay leaves**
	1/2 tsp	**Fennel** ground
	1 pinch	**Saffron**
4. Add and **cook for 5 minutes:**	2 lbs	**White fish**
5. Add and cook until all shells are open:	16	**Clams***
	16	**Mussels***
	16	**Shrimp**

5. ***Very Important:** *Remove clams or mussels that are tightly closed shut after cooking. This indicates they were dead before cooking and are inedible and harmful.*

Rouille

6. In a small pot mix until hot:	2 Tbs	**Olive oil**
	2 cups	**Whole wheat bread crumbs**
Spoon on top of soup when served.	1 cup	**Parmesan cheese**
	1/2 cup	**Water**
	1/8 tsp	**Cayenne**
	1/4 cup	**Fresh basil**

Summer Borsch

Serves 6

My mother's family came from St. Petersburg, Russia, and my grandmother was one of fourteen children who grew up near the city of Archangel. Archangel is located way up in the higher latitudes where it is very cold. My grandmother Rose eventually came to New York. She met her husband Morris there, and they had four children. Mother was the youngest and the only girl. This soup was their staple growing up, and we, her children, grew up on it as well. I have cooked it many times for my family and they all love it, even though each of my kids has very different tastes in food. This soup is referred to as borsht in some cookbooks, but my daughter Francesca, who lived in Russia for six years with her native Russian husband, explained that the word should be spelled the way you see here.

My family's borsch is served chilled, so it is most convenient to cook it one day ahead of time. The night before, I cook an extra amount of vegetables for dinner; that way I make two meals out of it, with plenty left over to make borsch the next day.

1. Steam in a very large pot until soft:
   Add to pot in the order given while cutting.
   Beets take the longest to cook.

   Save broth for soup.

6 cups	**Water**	
4 large	**Beets** cut into large bite-size pieces; include greens	
3 large	**Carrots** sliced	
2 large	**Onions** cut into large bite-size pieces	
8 large	**New potatoes** cut into large bite-size pieces	

2. Blend the vegetables in a blender with the broth. You may need to do this in two batches if your blender is small. If you find the proportion too dry for blending, add ½ cup extra liquid such as soup broth or water. The consistency should be thick and a little rough.

3. Mix into soup:

⅓ cup	**Lemon** juiced
½ tsp	**Salt**
	Pepper to taste
1 tsp	**Paprika**

4. Serve chilled and garnish with:

1 cup	**Yogurt** or **sour cream**
4	**Eggs** hardboiled and cut into pieces
2	**Green onions** chopped

Avocado and Cucumber Soup

.... *Serves 6* ....

This soup is great as a little appetizer to a summer meal of corn, fresh bread, and tomato salad.

1. Blend in blender:

2	**Cucumbers** peeled and cut
1	**Avocado** cut into small pieces
2 cloves	**Garlic**
2	**Green onions**
3/4 cup	**Water**
1/2	**Lemon** juiced

2. Then add, and blend:

1/8 tsp	**Salt**
1 dash	**Pepper**
1/8 tsp	**Paprika**

3. Serve chilled with:

2	**Green onions** chopped

4. Serve with a dollop on top of each serving:

1 cup	**Yogurt** or **sour cream**

5. Garnish with:

4 Tbs	**Cilantro** chopped

Marica's Gazpacho

This soup is great for a hot summer evening.

1. Blend in blender:

8 large	**Tomatoes** fresh
2 cloves	**Garlic**

2. Pour into a large bowl and add:

2	**Red peppers** chopped small
1	**Cucumber** diced
1	**Red onion** chopped small
2	**Avocados** cubed
1^1/2 cups	**Corn** freshly cut off the cob
4 Tbs	**Vinegar** or **lemon juice**
1^1/2 tsp	**Cumin** ground
	Salt and **pepper** to taste

3. Sprinkle a little over each serving:
Served chilled.

1 bunch	**Cilantro** chopped

Poor Man's Gazpacho

This soup is a recipe straight from Spain. Mary, Enrico's sister, married a man from Spain. They spent the first three years of their life together there, and she came home with some great recipes. This one is simple and very tasty. It is typical of southeastern Spain.

1. Blend in blender starting at a low speed, finishing on high:

8 large	**Tomatoes**
3 cloves	**Garlic**
1 cup	**Water**
1 slice	**Old bread**
2^1/2 Tbs	**Olive oil**
1^1/2 Tbs	**Balsalmic vinegar**
	Salt and **pepper** to taste

2. Sprinkle a little over each serving:
Served chilled.

1 bunch	**Parsley** chopped

Yogurt Soup

······························ *Serves 6* ······························

This soup is very easy and quick. It is especially nice
on a hot summer night.

In a large bowl combine:

2	**Cucumbers** cubed
¼ cup	**Radishes** sliced thin
2 cups	**Yogurt**
1 cup	**Water** or **soup stock**
1 Tbs	**Fresh mint**
1 dash	**Salt** and **pepper**

Serve chilled.

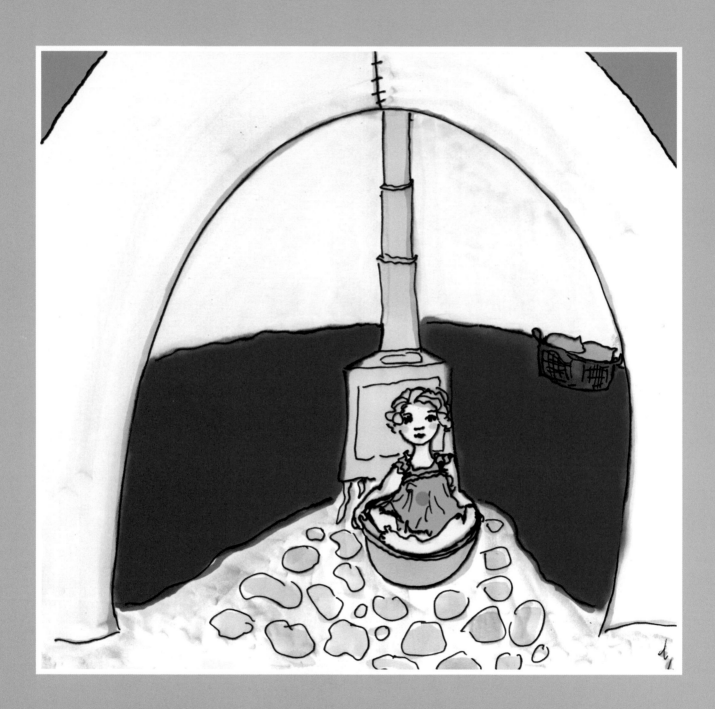

Our Teepee

It made a cozy home. A raised wooden platform surrounded a small but efficient wood-burning stove. Flat river rocks made a floor under the stove and held the heat. A short chimney pipe popped up about four feet above the stove, and a smoke hole at the top of the teepee sucked out the smoke. Adjustable smoke flaps helped direct the smoke up and out depending on the direction of the wind. We put a dark orange carpet down on the platform and often sat around the wood-burning stove on the step it created. I was always surprised how many people we could accommodate in that small space, as many as fifteen people at one time.

We took the little kitchen stove and sink unit out of the trailer and placed it on the platform on one side. Eventually we piped water from the river upstream. To cook or wash dishes I had to kneel, which made my knees protest. Kitchen items were neatly placed around the edge of the platform where it was too low to sit without hitting your head.

Nearby we put a pretty blue and white cotton cloth on the rug, which created a dining area. At night we lit candled lanterns that we hung from the poles all around the teepee. On the other side was a rocking chair that I had had in the trailer for nursing Marica. Behind it we kept books and toys, creating a living room area. Directly in front, on the other side of the wood stove, was our king-size futon, which snugly held all four of us. Our stove kept us warm through a good part of the night, but Enrico usually got up and added wood toward morning. The long poles that supported the teepee were lodge pole pines, and along their length were little knots that caught rain, which then dripped on us, our bed, and other places. When it rained during the winter months, we had to cover the foot of the bed with plastic so we didn't get too wet.

Normally, if the rain wasn't too intense, after a day or two of dampness and mud, things dried out pretty fast. Being pregnant, I was nauseous and unusually sensitive to smells. When the weather was bad, mice would crawl in at night while we slept and sometimes tickle our faces. Although the mouse droppings were an irritant, their urine was worse because it was impossible to locate. As time went on it was difficult to get rid of the smell and I got pretty impatient for our house to be finished. We liked the setup in the teepee so much that we designed the house to be similar. Just after we moved into the house, Andrei was born.

Our house is rectangular, primarily one large room with an open loft above, a little room in each back corner below, and a bathroom in the middle of the back wall. The house faces south, with an overhang that keeps the sun out in the summer but allows it to come through the large sliding glass doors during the winter. It warms up our Mexican paver tiles and the inch-thick cement underneath. Our only other source of heat is a wood-burning stove in a well in the middle of the house, surrounded by wooden steps in the shape of an octagon. The kitchen area is on one side with windows all along the counter. There are no cabinets by choice, and we keep our dishes in drawers below. We sit Japanese style on buckwheat pillows on a large cozy rug around the low dining table.

In the early days, we all slept above in the loft. At first, we had a lineup of mattresses on the floor. Gradually, as the children got older, we put up bookshelf partitions, creating four separate areas. Successively, each child moved down to one of the little rooms in the corners of the house. Then when the oldest moved out, the next one took over that space. The children loved our setup when they were young. When they were upstairs, they could see me in the kitchen and I could hear what was going on. I was always available and that made them feel safe. However, as they entered into their teens they began to resent the setup. Although I knew I would hear complaints as the kids got older, we never seemed to figure out an effective transition.

Salads and Dressings

Frankie's Salad Dressing

·········· *Serves 6* ··········

My mother used to make this salad dressing at the dinner table. It was a whole ritual. Each evening she was handed the various ingredients on a small tray, and she would pour them into a little yellow metal bowl. Then she would stir it fast with a wooden spoon, tapping a few drops on her wrist to test-taste it, adding whatever was needed before pouring it over the whole salad. It was always delicious, with slight variations that gave it its charm. It is one you would never tire of. Friends would always ask her for the recipe. Be sure to use the best quality ingredients because that is the secret of her dressing.

In a small bowl mix together:

6 Tbs	**Extra virgin olive oil**
3 Tbs	**Vinegar** balsamic is preferred
2 tsp	**Tarragon** dried
2 cloves	**Garlic** pressed
	Salt and **pepper** to taste

Blue Heron Salad Dressing

Serves 6

I don't follow any ritual when I make this dressing. I discovered that you can pour each ingredient on top of the lettuce and it doesn't seem to make any difference. Try it both ways. It's funny but my friends tend to ask me for this recipe too. However, I have made a few changes. Again, be sure to use the best ingredients because that is the real secret to its wonderful taste.

In a small bowl mix together:

3 Tbs	**Extra virgin olive oil**
3 Tbs	**Flax oil**
3 Tbs	**Balsamic vinegar**
1 tsp	**Dill**
1 Tbs	**Ginger** minced
	Salt and **pepper** to taste

Baby Green Salad

Careful drying of the lettuce leaves is very important because the remaining water dilutes the salad dressing. Do not squeeze the delicate leaves. Use a towel to dab dry. This salad you can eat daily and never tire of.

In a very large salad bowl mix:

2 heads	**Red lettuce** washed and dried
1 handful	**Baby greens** washed and dried

Wonderful options to add:

2 large	**Tomatoes** sliced
1	**Avocado** sliced
1	**Cucumber** sliced
1	**Red pepper** sliced
1 bunch	**Arugula**

Optional: **¼ cup Goat cheese** sprinkled on top

Serve with **Frankie's Salad Dressing,** page 94 or **Blue Heron Salad Dressing,** page 95.

Sackets Harbor Summer Salad

Serves 6

This is one of our favorite salads in the summer. We usually serve this with corn freshly picked out of the garden. During the summer season we eat this meal several times a week.

In a large flat dish arrange in a pattern:

6 large	**Tomatoes** sliced thin
2 large	**Cucumbers** sliced thin
1 medium	**Red onion** sliced thin
1	**Avocado** sliced
¼ cup	**Fresh basil**

Oil and Vinegar Dressing

3 Tbs	**Olive oil**
1 Tbs	**Balsamic vinegar**
½ tsp	**Dill**
	Salt and **pepper** to taste

Santa Barbara Salad Variation

Serves 6

In a large flat dish arrange in a pattern:

2 lbs	**Mozzarella cheese** fresh
4 large	**Tomatoes** fresh and tasty
4 Tbs	**Capers**
1 bunch	**Basil**
1 cup	**Mixed olives** good quality

Oil and Vinegar Dressing

½ cup	**Olive oil**
2 Tbs	**Balsamic vinegar**
	Salt and **pepper** to taste

Cool Cucumber Salad

This side dish is one of my favorites. It is so versatile that you can put it in sandwiches or have it with dinner. The salad is elegant and simple and a great addition to almost any meal.

1. In a medium shallow bowl place the following ingredients:

1 large	**Cucumber** sliced very thin
1/2	**Red onion** sliced very thin
2 Tbs	**Rice vinegar**
1 Tbs	**Lime** or **lemon** juiced
1/8 tsp	**Salt**

2. Toss the above ingredients and add:

| 1 tsp | **Dill** sprinkled on top |

Potato and Bell Pepper Salad

Serves 6

This potato salad is different and simply delicious. It is great with new potatoes.

1. In a large pot with a steamer, cook:

2 cups	**Water** enough to cover bottom of steamer
8	**New potatoes** diced in large pieces
2	**Red peppers** diced in large pieces
2	**Green peppers** diced in large pieces
2	**Yellow onions** diced in large pieces

2. Steam until potatoes are just soft, **about 20 minutes.**

3. Drain into a large bowl and let cool to room temperature. The stock can be used for soup.

Dressing

In a separate bowl make salad dressing, or just pour each ingredient over salad and stir:

6 Tbs	**Olive oil**
3 Tbs	**Vinegar**
1 Tbs	**Dill**
	Salt and **pepper** to taste

Mixed Bean Salad

Serves 6

Bean salad is a wonderful way of using up cooked leftover beans.
This salad has been used in our Zen retreats, along with Baby Green
Salad on page 96 and Rice Salad on page 101, on a warm day at lunch.

1. In a large bowl mix:

4 cups	**Cooked beans** $1^1/3$ cup of each: kidney, black, Anasazi
2 large	**Red onions** diced
2 large	**Tomatoes** diced
1/2 cup	**Cilantro** chopped

2. Cook separately:

4 cobs	**Corn** cooked and cut off the cob

Dressing

4 Tbs	**Olive oil**
2 Tbs	**Balsamic vinegar**
2 cloves	**Garlic** crushed
	Salt and **pepper** to taste

Rice Salad

This salad is wonderful with leftovers especially when you have people visiting for a few days.

In a large bowl mix:

2 cups	**Brown** or **white rice** cooked
1	**Cucumber** cubed
1	**Tomato** fresh, cubed
1	**Red pepper** diced
1	**Green pepper** diced
1	**Red onion** diced
¼ cup	**Cilantro** or **parsley**
¼ tsp	**Salt**

Dressing

2 Tbs	**Rice vinegar**
4 Tbs	**Apple juice**
1 Tbs	**Tamari** soy sauce
1 Tbs	**Olive oil**

My Roasted Red Bell Peppers

This is a favorite of mine. I use a few strips in salads and on sandwiches with melted cheese or goat cheese.

1. In a large buttered baking dish place:

12	**Red bell peppers** whole

2. Place up high in oven and bake at **450°** **for 20 minutes**.

3. Turn them over after the tops blister, **about 15 minutes**.

4. Remove from oven and let cool.
   Peel the thin skins and remove inside seeds while rinsing under cold water.

5. Slice the peppers in long strips and put in a bowl or large glass jar.

6. Cover peppers with:

½ cup	**Olive oil**
4 cloves	**Garlic** minced

7. Refrigerate and use a few strips at a time.
   Store refrigerated up to two weeks.

   Serve with:
   Goat Cheese Salad *on page 103*
   Baby Green Salad *on page 96*

Goat Cheese Salad

This is wonderful with beans and a green salad.

In a medium bowl place the following:	8 oz	**Goat cheese**
	3 Tbs	**Olive oil** poured over the cheese and mixed just slightly
	¼ cup	**Fresh oregano** stems removed or **1 Tbs dried oregano**
Option:	¼ cup	**Roasted red peppers** thinly sliced and arranged on top

Serve with:
Blue Heron Beans *on page 31*
Baby Green Salad *on page 96*

Cloved Fruit Compote

I always serve compote for breakfast along with cereal and eggs during sesshins, our meditation retreats. It is warm and tasty poured over cereal.

1. Bring to a boil in a medium pot:

1 cup	Water

2. Cut into bite-size pieces and add:
    (Remember, they swell
    up when cooked.)

6	**Dried pears**
6	**Dried apricots**
6	**Dried peaches**
6	**Dried apples**
6	**Dried prunes** remove pits
6	**Whole cloves**
2 pieces	**Crystallized ginger** cut into smaller pieces

Reduce heat and cook for 1/2 hour.

Two Fruit Salads

Fruit salad is served as a complete dinner in our home in the warm months. It is better to use only three or four fruits at a time to really enjoy them and of course it is wonderful to use what is in season. Below are two combinations I recommend.

#1. In a medium bowl mix:

4 cups	**Strawberries**
4	**Oranges** peeled and sliced, or substitute tangerine pieces; they come in little cans and are great for a change
4	**Bananas** sliced
1 cup	**Orange juice**
1 cup	**Apple juice**

#2. Another great combination:

2 cups	**Blueberries**
8	**Peaches** peeled and sliced
4	**Bananas** sliced
1 cup	**Apple juice**
1 cup	**Orange juice**

Serve with:
Yogurt or **cottage cheese**
Almonds
Granola
Maple syrup

Raita Salad

······· *Serves 6* ·······

This is a yogurt salad that is usually eaten with spicy Indian food.
However, it is wonderful on a hot day with any meal.

1. In a large bowl mix:

2 cups	**Yogurt**
6	**Cucumbers** grated fine; squeeze out juice before adding to yogurt
3 Tbs	**Mint** fresh or $1/2$ tsp dried

2. Garnish with:

3	**Green onions** chopped

Fire

Very early on, Enrico and I established that we needed three things before we started building a house. We needed a workshop so we would have a place to work from. Enrico wanted a backhoe for heavy clearing and roadwork. We wanted a reservoir, a 20,000 gallon body of water, for fire fighting. We situated the reservoir against the hill, fed by the natural spring way up on the mountain, so we could have strong gravity flow. Below, we put in a fire pump, and we bought some actual fire hoses. We began hacking away the brush to create a fuel break around our house and workshop. Some people laughed at us for being overly cautious, but we knew we couldn't rest unless we were protected. It turned out we were not being too vigilant. We had our first fire scare in 1983. Our neighbor down at the gate decided to conduct a controlled burn at his ranch, only a mile from us, to clear brush. Firefighters were there to help. The Forest Service encourages periodic controlled burns to reduce the fire hazard by reducing the amount of available fuel.

A few hours after the controlled burn started, we watched from a midpoint between our house and his, between the two rivers. As I ran home for some drinking water, I saw that the fire had jumped both rivers and the wind was blowing it toward our house. I ran back down to tell the fire chief, and he said, "Everything is under control, ma'am." I waited a few moments before repeating, "The fire is on our side, over there."

He ignored me. This happened a couple more times. Enrico and I looked at each other, silently asking, Why doesn't he believe us? Another neighbor who had driven up behind us tried a more straightforward tactic. "Damn it, you aren't listening! The fire is spreading toward their house."

Disbelieving, the fire chief answered, "Okay, okay, just a minute . . . I'll take a look." He walked in the direction we pointed, disappeared from sight for a moment, and then came running back. His walkie-talkie was in his hand and he was urgently requesting backup and fire bombers, airplanes that drop chemicals to retard flames. He barely apologized to us.

At home, only a half-mile away, we were prepared; we had already taken out all our hoses and tested our fire system. As the fire licked the brush a quarter-mile from our house, in an amazing stroke of good fortune, the wind changed. We didn't end up using our fire hoses that time. But we did just two years later.

The Santa Ana was blowing early in the summer of 1985. The witch's wind, they call it. It's a strong, gusty, dry wind charged with positive ions, which affect people emotionally. The wind causes irritability, and in some cases even leads to violence. We noticed smoke rising in the mountains to the east. It looked fairly dense, which meant it wasn't too far away—maybe three miles as the crow flies.

The winds were blowing from the west, so our chances still looked good at that point. Even so, a deputy sheriff awakened us at 2:00 in the morning. The officer told us that they were evacuating everyone in the area. We gathered the kids and the dogs, grabbed important papers, a few clothes, and the children's favorite stuffed animals, and left to spend what little remained of the night with friends in town.

Early the next morning Enrico and the dogs returned to turn off the propane and check the fire's progress. There was a roadblock at the mouth of the canyon, about six miles from our ranch. The whole of Matilija Canyon was closed off, with police and fire personnel strictly enforcing the closure. Homeowners were allowed to drive through but only at their own risk. The fire was burning the edges of the road, but it had not yet reached our place. Enrico was surprised to find two friends waiting at our ranch, ready to help protect our home. Hal and Robert often hiked the trails near our property, and when they heard the fire threatened the area, they'd managed to sneak past the barricade to help fight it. Since we did not have a telephone at the time, Enrico was unable to tell me of his change of plans, and I was left wondering what had happened to him.

Later that afternoon I drove as far as the roadblock. I requested they send in a helicopter to check on the condition of my husband. I was turned away. "My husband's in there," I protested. "I don't know whether he's dead or alive." The firefighters were very polite but refused to make any moves. They explained that the thick smoke and gusty winds made flying conditions too dangerous. I turned my car around and spent a long second night with my three children in a strange place near town; they had trouble sleeping through the excitement, and so we stayed up to watch the flames curling up the mountain.

The next morning, Vincenzo, Enrico's sixteen-year-old son, was to arrive at the Los Angeles airport from Toronto. I had to leave to pick him up with no knowledge of what had happened to Enrico at the ranch. Meanwhile, Enrico, Hal, and Robert were preparing for the approaching fire. The three of them made plans to back-burn, a strategy of purposely burning the hills around homes. The back-burn flames rise up and away from the homesite, clearing out the highly flammable underbrush and leaving much less for the forest fire to burn.

First they set out hoses, placing them near the house and workshop. They then watered everything down, all around and on top of the structures. They kept watering until they saw the flames coming down the mountainside toward them. Then they back-burned. Robert grabbed a torch and ran along the base of the mountains, setting them afire. Enrico got worried because he didn't return. In the smoke and confusion, Robert lost his bearings and couldn't find his way back. He became trapped in a ring of his own fire. It was much later when, to their relief, the other two saw him wandering in a daze down the hill to the house. Meanwhile, Enrico and Hal continued hosing down the house and workshop. There was so much smoke and heat that they didn't know when the fire actually hit. They had intended to go in the house and lie on the floor with a wet covering over them at the critical point, but not knowing when the fire hit, they just kept watering. It wasn't until the air cleared a little that they realized the fire had passed through.

The children and I arrived in Los Angeles just in time to meet Vincenzo, who as a teenager found our story exciting and frightening. We were all worried about Enrico and wondered whether our home was intact. When we got to Ojai, police officers and firefighters at the base of Matilija Canyon told us we couldn't go in. I said I had to see if my husband was alive and my home still there, and they let us pass. We began driving at a crawl through an unfamiliar and strange landscape, a scene out of a sci-fi film. Along the sides of the road, areas of the fire were still blazing. I accelerated past those places, closing my eyes for a second and hoping we could slip by the orange flames. The sky became redder and redder as we neared our home. The trees were blackened, their branches grotesquely twisted and bare.

When we finally got home the dogs came up to us wagging their tails, and I cried. I ran down to the house. Our home and workshop were untouched and Enrico, Robert, and Hal were all there, sooty and dazed. Our three heroes! We all hugged and cried and looked around in disbelief. Our place was an island amid twisted charcoal stumps and black ash that covered the ground as far as the eye could see.

We celebrated being alive and together again. Later, looking around our transformed land, we realized that the fire had cleared out all the brush for us.

Breads and Muffins

Whole Wheat Bread

This bread is very healthy and delicious. We made it consistently for many years. We even ground our own red winter wheat. Since the children have grown and we are doing other things, it seems harder to find the time but it is very well worth your while. There is nothing like eating a slice of bread just out of the oven with a little butter. Our family would finish off a half loaf just minutes after it finished baking.

1. In a large saucepan heat until about 110° or test a few drops on your wrist:

2 cups	**Water**
2 cups	**Milk** or **soy milk**
¼ cup	**Honey**

2. Pour into large bowl and add by sprinkling on top:
Do **not** stir. Cover and keep warm until yeast foams (**about 5–10 minutes**).

2¼ tsp	**Dry yeast** (1 package)

3. Add:

3 Tbs	**Olive oil**
9 cups	**Whole wheat flour**
½ tsp	**Salt**

Do not put total amount in at once.
Add as follows:
   5 cups flour and stir well;
   then 2 more,
   then 1,
   then 1/2 (save last half).
   Pour onto large wooden board
   dusted with some flour,
   then add last 1/2 cup of flour.

4. Knead bread on a large board and add a little flour at a time if it gets too sticky. Work the dough by pushing and folding, then turn the dough over and make a 1/4 turn. Push again continuing the sequence until springy, about **10 minutes.**

5. Place in a large lightly oiled bowl and cover. **Let rise for 1 hour in a warm place.**

6. Punch dough down in the bowl, turn over. **Let rise again for 1/2 hour.**

   Preheat oven to 350°.

7. Roll dough out onto the board and divide into four equal parts. Make into loaf shapes and place in buttered bread pans.

8. Let rise just **5 minutes** in warm place.

9. Gently rub a little milk or soy milk on top surface for a more golden crust.

   Bake at 350° for 45 minutes.
   To test if bread is done, tap bottom and listen for a hollow sound.

Optional choices:
1. You can make variations by adding:
   2 Tbs Caraway seeds or
   1/4 cup Sesame seeds or
   1/4 cup Cracked wheat

2. You can exchange: **1/2 cup Whole wheat flour** for **1/2 cup Rye flour.** With this variation you can add **1 Tbs Rosemary** as well.

Try any or all of these ideas, or experiment with your own.

Rosemary Corn Bread

Makes 3 loaves

Corn bread is one of our favorites with soup when you want a change from wheat bread. It is so easy to make and you feel as though it's special when you offer it. I like it with soup that has beans or tomatoes in it, and I like to serve it with a large salad.

Preheat oven to 350°.

1. In a large bowl add and mix in order given:

3 Tbs	**Butter** melted
5	**Eggs**
1/2 cup	**Milk** or **soy milk**
1 1/2 cups	**Yogurt**
1/3 cup	**Honey** or **maple syrup**
2 tsp	**Rosemary** minced
1 1/2 cups	**White flour** or **whole wheat flour** or **spelt flour**
2 1/4 cups	**Cornmeal**
1 1/2 tsp	**Baking powder**
3/4 tsp	**Baking soda**
1/2 tsp	**Salt**

2. Use three buttered bread pans.

    Bake at 350° for 30 minutes or until golden brown.

Garlic Bread

Here you may want to buy French bread and serve with spaghetti or hot soup.

1. Slice at 1-inch intervals but not all the way through:

2 loaves	**French bread**

2. In a small pan melt together:

8 Tbs	**Butter** unsalted
4 cloves	**Fresh garlic** crushed
$^1/_2$ tsp	**Garlic powder***
1 pinch	**Salt**

3. Paint each side of the slices of bread with butter mixture.

4. Wrap each loaf with aluminum foil.

Bake at 350° for 20 minutes.

* I sometimes use instead: *Spice Hunter's Spicy Garlic Seasoning*

Tortillas from South America

Makes 6

This is a recipe from Francesca. And it's great too.

1. In a medium bowl mix together:
   Let sit for 30 minutes.

2 cups	**Water**
3 Tbs	**Olive oil**
4¹/₂ cups	**Whole wheat flour** or **2 cups whole wheat and 2¹/₂ cups white flour**
¹/₈ tsp	**Salt**

2. Break apart dough into six balls. Roll out each ball of dough on a floured wooden board until flat and thin like a tortilla.

   Cook on a dry skillet for **2 minutes per side** over medium heat or until small brown spots appear.

Naan from India

Makes 6

These are a little puffier and softer than tortillas.

1. In a large bowl mix together with your hands until it forms a sponge ball:

4 cups	**Spelt white flour** or **white flour**
3 Tbs	**Butter** melted
1¹/₂ cups	**Yogurt**
¹/₄ cup	**Warm water**
¹/₂ tsp	**Salt**
1 tsp	**Baking powder**

2. Let sit for ³/₄ hour covered with a damp cloth. **Preheat oven to 500°** or use broiler.

3. Pull apart dough into six balls.

4. Roll out each ball of dough on a floured wooden board until flat and a little thicker than a tortilla. Cook only one side on a dry skillet over medium heat **3–5 minutes** until brown spots appear. Place naan directly on rack in **hot oven for 1 minute** until top is golden brown.

5. Brush melted butter on top on each naan. You can add garlic to the melted butter.

Banana Bread

.... *Makes 2 loaves* ....

My kids loved banana bread and loved to help make it. They would all
gather around me and take turns adding ingredients.

Preheat oven to 350°.

1. In a large bowl combine:

4		**Eggs**
8	Tbs	**Butter** (1 stick) melted
1/2	cup	**Honey**
2	tsp	**Vanilla**
4	drops	**Almond extract**
4 or 5		**Bananas** mashed
1/2	cup	**Milk** or **soy milk**

2. In a separate bowl mix and
   add to wet ingredients:

3 1/2	cups	**Whole wheat flour**
4	tsp	**Baking powder**
1/4	tsp	**Nutmeg**
1/8	tsp	**Cinnamon**
1	pinch	**Salt**

3. Butter and pour batter
   into two bread pans.

   Bake at 325° for 50 minutes.

Weiner Sisters' Popovers

Toby Weiner and her daughters, Deborah and Jessica, gave this recipe to our family. Popovers are an unusual treat. They need to be eaten immediately, so plan accordingly.

Preheat oven to 450°.
Butter a muffin pan and lightly flour.

1. In a medium bowl mix until smooth:

2	cups	**White flour**
2	cups	**Milk**
1/8	tsp	**Salt**
2	Tbs	**Butter** melted

2. Add one egg at a time. Stir fast and immediately fill buttered muffin pans. Fill cups 3/4 full.

4		**Eggs** (do not over beat)

3. **Bake at 450° for 15 minutes.**
   Reduce heat to 375° and bake for
   20 more minutes.
   Do not open oven during baking time!

4. After baking, pierce with a sharp knife to release steam.

   Serve immediately.

Golden Scones

Marica loves to bake, and this is one of her favorites. Scones are great anytime with a fresh cup of tea or coffee. Feel free to substitute fresh fruit or any favorite dry fruits that you love.

Preheat oven to 350°.

1. In a medium bowl combine:

4¼ cups	White flour
4 tsp	Baking powder
2 Tbs	Sugar
¼ tsp	Salt
1	Orange rind grated

2. Cut into above mixture:
   Crumble in with fingers until it resembles crumbs.

8 Tbs	Butter (1 stick) cold

3. Add:

¾ cup	Currants

4. In a separate bowl whisk and add to flour mixture stirring in gently:

4	Eggs

5. Add:

¾ cup	Coconut milk or regular milk

6. Turn onto wooden cutting board, roll out, and cut into circles or triangles.
   Do not overwork the dough.

7. Place on a large buttered cookie sheet.

Bake at 350° for 25 minutes.

Marica's Biscuits

.... *Serves 6* ....

This is Marica's recipe. And it's great. For a fluffier biscuit use
only white flour.

Preheat oven to 375°.

1. In a medium bowl mix together:

4 cups	**White** or **whole wheat flour**
1/2 tsp	**Salt**
2 Tbs	**Baking powder**
2 tsp	**Sugar**

2. Add and crumble with your fingers until it resembles coarse crumbs:

10 Tbs	**Butter**

3. Add and mix gently with your hands until it holds together and forms a ball:

1 cup	**Whipping cream***
1/2 cup	**Water***

4. Roll out to 3/4-inch thick and cut into triangle shapes, or use a drinking glass to cut into circles.

*or substitute 3/4 cup yogurt and 3/4 cup water.

5. Place on a buttered cookie sheet.

Bake at 375° for 20 minutes
or until golden.

Quick Ginger Molasses Muffins

Makes 12 muffins

Muffins like these are easy and a sure thing. The apple sauce in them is wonderful. We like to eat these muffins with Brie cheese.

Preheat oven to 350°.

1. In a large bowl combine:

4	**Eggs**
4 Tbs	**Butter** melted
½ cup	**Sugar**
½ cup	**Milk** or **soy milk**
¾ cup	**Molasses**
1 cup	**Apple sauce**
1 tsp	**Vanilla**
2 Tbs	**Ginger** minced

2. In a separate bowl mix and then add to wet ingredients:

2 cups	**Whole wheat flour**
½ tsp	**Cinnamon**
⅛ tsp	**Cardamom**
⅛ tsp	**Nutmeg**
2 tsp	**Baking powder**
1 pinch	**Salt**

3. Butter muffin baking tin and pour each cup ½ full.

Bake at 350° for 20–30 minutes.

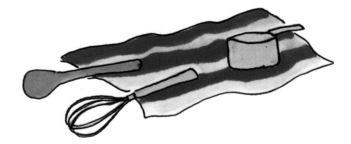

Breakfast

Sunday Pancakes

······················· *Serves 6* ·······················

When the children were young we had pancakes often. Nowadays it's a special treat when we get together and have them for breakfast. Once in a while I serve these pancakes for dinner; they are so healthy, a full meal in themselves.

1. In a medium bowl mix together in order given:

8	**Eggs**
3 Tbs	**Butter** melted
2 cups	**Milk** or **soy milk**
2 cups	**Yogurt**
2 tsp	**Vanilla**

2. Add all at once on top of egg mixture and stir:

1/8 tsp	**Nutmeg**
1/8 tsp	**Salt**
2 Tbs	**Orange rind** grated
4 1/4 cups	**Whole wheat flour**
4 tsp	**Baking powder**
3	**Bananas** small cubes

3. Heat and butter a heavy-duty skillet and use a 1/4-cup measure to pour the batter onto the skillet.

Serve with: **Maple syrup**
Yogurt
Apple sauce
Fresh berries

Hearty Breakfast Crepes

This is one of my favorites. I love the delicacy of crepes and the variety of fillings you can use. You will need a large flat skillet. Butter the pan well. Preheat pan on medium heat so that a drop of water balls up.

1. Mix in a medium bowl:

1 cup	**Whole wheat flour**
1 cup	**White flour**
1 pinch	**Salt**

2. Add gradually to avoid lumps:

2^1/2 cups	**Milk** or **soy milk**
^{1}/2 tsp	**Vanilla**
4 Tbs	**Butter** melted

3. Add one at a time to avoid lumping:

9	**Eggs**

4. Pour ^{1}/3 cup batter onto the heated skillet. Tip skillet around so that the batter spreads evenly over the entire pan. Cook until small brown spots appear, **about 2 minutes**. Flip over and cook for a few more seconds until done.

5. Roll crepes up with your favorite filling, cover with a dish towel, and place them in a warm oven to keep warm.

Suggested fillings:
Jam
Apple sauce
Bananas
Apricots cooked
Ice cream and nuts

Be creative!

Delectable French Toast

We often use light whole wheat, sourdough, or challah bread that is a little old, but any bread that you like will work. The secret to good French toast? Be sure to let the bread soak; this gives it a wonderful moist texture.

1. Mix in a medium bowl then transfer to a flat casserole dish:

8	**Eggs**
3 cups	**Milk** or **soy milk**
1 Tbs	**Maple syrup**
1 tsp	**Vanilla**
1 Tbs	**Orange rind** grated
¼ tsp	**Nutmeg**
1 pinch	**Salt**

2. Cut into thick slices:

1 loaf	**Bread** large

3. Dunk bread pieces into batter until soaked.

4. On a buttered skillet over a medium-low heat, cook each piece until nicely brown, then turn over and brown on other side. Place in a warm oven to keep them warm.

Serve with: **Maple syrup**
Yogurt
Berries

 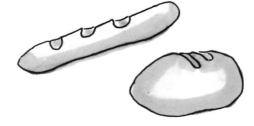

Birthday Waffles

.... *Serves 4* ....

Enrico gave Marica an electric waffle iron for her birthday one year and it made a world of difference. We used to have a cast-iron stove-top griddle but found the electric model easier because the waffles wouldn't stick.

1. Mix in a medium bowl:

3	**Eggs**
1½ cups	**Milk** or **soy milk**
4 Tbs	**Butter** melted
2 Tbs	**Maple syrup**
1½ tsp	**Vanilla**
1 pinch	**Nutmeg**
⅛ tsp	**Salt**

2. Mix into above mixture:

2¼ cups	**Whole wheat flour**
1 Tbs	**Baking powder**

3. Butter waffle iron well each time.

4. Cook until golden brown. Place in a warm oven to keep them warm.

Serve with: **Maple syrup**
Fresh fruit

Sesshin Oatmeal

Oatmeal is a favorite hot cereal for many people. To add a little flavor we serve it with compote during our meditation retreats.

1. In a medium pot combine and heat over a low flame:

3 cups	**Oatmeal**
3 cups	**Water**
3 cups	**Milk** or **soy milk**
¼ tsp	**Salt**
¼ tsp	**Nutmeg**

2. Stir often and cook over low heat until thick (about 10 minutes). Turn off heat. Cover and let stand for a few minutes before serving.

Serve with: **Milk** or **soy milk**
Compote
Granola
Maple syrup

Early Morning Rice Cream

Serves 6

This is a hot porridge or cereal that is particularly good if you make it yourself. If you have a grain or coffee grinder then you can start from scratch. If not, you can buy the rice cream in your health food store and pan-fry it.

1. In a medium, dry pot on low heat, stir until browned:

1 cup	Rice granules* (rice cream cereal)

2. Add and stir often on low heat until thick:

It takes a while to thicken—give it time.

2¹/₂ cups	Milk or **soy milk**
2¹/₂ cups	Water
¹/₄ tsp	Nutmeg
¹/₈ tsp	Salt

3. Stir often. Turn off heat, cover, and let stand 10 minutes.

Serve with:
Milk or **soy milk**
Maple syrup
Bananas or **compote**

You can pan-toast your own uncooked brown rice in a large pan until slightly browned and then grind coarsely in a grain grinder.

Home-Baked Granola

Serves 8

This is a nice amount but you might go through it fast if you like granola. I usually make twice this amount. This granola is wonderful with fruit salad and yogurt and with a little maple syrup on top. We sometimes have this for supper on a hot summer evening over fresh fruit salad.

Preheat oven to 350°.

1. In a large bowl combine:

8 cups	**Oatmeal**
1 cup	**Almonds**
1 cup	**Cashews**
1 cup	**Pecans** or **walnuts**
1 cup	**Coconut**
1	**Orange rind** grated

2. In a small bowl mix together then add to the large bowl:

¼ cup	**Coconut oil**
1¼ cups	**Apple juice**
1 tsp	**Vanilla**

Stir all ingredients right away, otherwise the oatmeal gets soggy.

3. Spread thinly onto two large cookie sheets and bake.

   Bake at 350° for 30 minutes or until browned. **Check every 10 minutes** and stir the granola so it gets browned evenly.

4. Add after baking:

1 cup	**Dried blueberries** or **cranberries**

Homeschooling

Francesca was five when we enrolled her at the private Oak Grove School in Ojai. The first year there was valuable and Francesca flourished. However, the following year she became bored with the classes, and we wondered what to do.

I was surprised when Enrico suggested we homeschool her, along with a classmate whose family was temporarily living on our property, but decided that it was worth a try. We came up with the idea that each parent would take one day a week and offer his or her particular interest or talent to the children. Sometimes we had cooking class, and Enrico liked to take them on hikes. The other parents offered projects on their days. This program lasted maybe two months, until the other little girl was clear that she wanted to return to school. Enrico and I decided to continue to homeschool, but we dropped our structure.

I remember walking into a local homeschool program in town early that fall and checking out their books. My heart sank. There was no way I could do what they suggested or follow their curriculum. Feeling overwhelmed and inadequate, I momentarily spiraled into depths of insecurity. But within a couple of hours I was telling myself, "Wait a minute, maybe this is for people who have no idea what to do. I don't need this, in fact it's an insult to my intelligence," and I resumed our home lessons with renewed energy. I found lessons were an invisible part of our every day, and there was no need to impose anything artificial. Our life on the ranch managed to offer lessons without the extra effort to do all the curriculum had suggested. Our only change was to emphasize the educational aspect of our life and to include projects and walks every day.

Francesca, who was six now, and Marica, two, were finding imaginative ways to entertain themselves. We had no television and didn't miss it, feeling it would have interfered with their ability to be resourceful. They often joined us in our projects or found their own. The children loved to draw and did it all the time. We read to them, and at some point I decided to teach them how to read. Enrico taught some math. I was amazed at the different learning styles each one had. Francesca was already able to read at four years, and by six was reading sophisticated material. She devoured books. Eventually, we had to restrict her reading to two hours a day. Marica wanted very badly to read as her big sister did, but it took her a couple of years to catch on. I know she felt frustrated and I was sorry she felt the need to emulate her older sister. But she did catch on by six or seven with no problem. Andrei was capable of reading quite early on but had no interest in it until he was eight years old, when suddenly he wanted to read building plans for model airplanes. It took a lot of restraint on my part to keep from pushing him before he was ready.

We managed to avoid a sense of isolation by taking the children to various activities in town. There were piano lessons and gymnastic classes. We joined a family singing group and put on a few shows with singing and dancing. The children made friends with other children they met at these activities and the friends would come to visit, often for days at a time. I felt as if our family had expanded.

Throughout the early years of homeschooling, I'd swing between feeling confident about the children's education and anxious about the value of our situation. Homeschooling was new in those days, and we didn't even follow the homeschool curriculum. However, both Enrico and I felt that if the condition of the world was an indication of how children were being raised and educated, we wanted to raise and educate ours differently. What was being offered in the world didn't impress us. We hoped that, because of their upbringing, our children would have confidence in their very bones, no matter what happened. Our kids got individual attention and hands-on experience that you cannot get in school. Yet we knew our unusual situation would cause hardship in unforeseen ways. The challenges of being different, not belonging, and perhaps being misunderstood might be hard to meet.

When the children were a little older, I opened a ballet school in town. Eventually, Francesca started teaching some of the younger classes and later Marica began to teach. But Ojai has a small population and expenses were high, and we eventually had to close down. Andrei didn't take part in the ballet but began playing tennis seriously and took fencing lessons for a number of years. When he was twelve, he and Enrico started taking glider lessons; both of them were always interested in flying. Despite our unconventional lifestyle and our constantly questioning whether we were taking the right path, those times were easy and very rewarding for all of us.

Puddings and Custards

Black Bear Apricot Pudding

Serves 6

Each spring, in late May, we get loads of apricots on our trees, so many we don't know what to do with them all. One year during a drought, a very bold, beautiful black bear paid us a visit. He would eat the fallen fruit as we sat and watched him. Our two dogs, Lupa and Pablo, would bark at the bear, but he would just look at them and keep eating.

1. In a medium-size pot cook down until soft, then drain:

4 cups	**Apricots** about 24 sliced
¼ cup	**Water**

2. Place on bottom of a 9 x 9-inch buttered bake dish:

1 cup	**Granola**

3. In a separate bowl combine:

6	**Eggs**
½ cup	**Honey**
2 cups	**Milk** or **soy milk**
2 tsp	**Vanilla**
¼ tsp	**Nutmeg**
¼ tsp	**Cinnamon**
¼ tsp	**Cardamom**

4. Add apricots to egg mixture and pour over granola.

Bake at 350° for 35 minutes.

Andrei's Favorite Bread Pudding

Serves 6

Bread pudding is a favorite with my whole family. If you have bread that is getting a little old, this is a great way to use it up. It's a healthy and filling dessert.

1. Tear into bite-size chunks and place in a large buttered 9 x 13-inch baking dish:

   ²/₃ loaf Whole wheat bread

2. In a large bowl combine:

8	**Eggs**
6 cups	**Milk** or **soy milk**
¹/₃ cup	**Maple syrup**
2 tsp	**Vanilla**
1	**Orange rind** grated
¹/₄ tsp	**Cardamom** ground
¹/₄ tsp	**Nutmeg** ground
¹/₈ tsp	**Cinnamon** ground

   Optional:

¹/₂ cup	**Raisins**
¹/₂ cup	**Coconut** grated

3. Pour liquid mixture over bread in baking pan.

   Bake at 350° for 40 minutes.

Brown Rice Custard

.... Serves 6 ....

This is a wonderful way to use up leftover brown rice.

Preheat oven to 350°.

1. In a large bowl mix all ingredients:

2. Butter an 8-inch square baking dish and fill with the rice mixture.

3. Place baking dish in a larger baking pan filled with an inch of water.

Bake for 55 minutes.

6	**Eggs**
3 cups	**Brown rice** precooked
2^1/2 cups	**Milk** or **soy milk**
^{1}/4 cup	**Raw sugar**
1^1/2 tsp	**Vanilla**
^{1}/2 tsp	**Cinnamon**
^{1}/3 cup	**Cranberries** dried
^{1}/3 cup	**Coconut** (optional)
1 pinch	**Salt**

Coconut Rice Pudding

Serves 6

This pudding is inspired by a rice pudding I had at a restaurant one time, but we use brown rice to make it a little healthier.

In a double boiler (one pot inside a larger one with 2 inches of water) mix together:

4 cups	**Soy milk** or **milk**
2 cups	**Coconut milk**
1 cup	**Brown sweet rice** or **brown rice**
1/3 cup	**Raw sugar** or **brown sugar**
1 cup	**Coconut** dried
1 Tbs	**Cardamom** whole
1/4 tsp	**Cinnamon** ground
1 pinch	**Salt**

Cook for 3–4 hours, stirring occasionally.

Mexican Rice Pudding

Serves 6

Javier and his family have been here for many years making our place beautiful. Aurelia, Javier's wife, showed me how to make this wonderful Mexican rice pudding that is a favorite of their family and ours.

In a large pot mix and **cook for 60 minutes** on medium heat, stirring occasionally:

1 cup	**White rice** uncooked
2 cups	**Milk**
6 cups	**Water**
1	**Cinnamon stick**
3 Tbs	**Sugar**
1 pinch	**Salt**

Optional: **1/2 cup Raisins**
1 cup Coconut

Mocha Mousse

Mocha Mousse was a rare treat when I was growing up. The mixture of coffee, chocolate, and cognac is brilliant.

1. In a small saucepan heat until melted: (You can use a medium-size bowl covered with plastic wrap and place in the microwave for one minute.)

½ lb	**Semisweet chocolate**
½ cup	**Coffee** strong (you can use decaf)

2. In a large 2½ quart bowl whip until pale yellow:

6	**Egg yolks*** (save egg whites)
½ cup	**Sugar**
1 tsp	**Vanilla**
2 Tbs	**Orange cognac** or **rum** (optional)

3. Pour chocolate-coffee mixture into egg-yolk mixture.

4. In separate medium bowl whip until stiff and fold into chocolate-egg mixture:

1 cup	**Cream** heavy

5. In another medium bowl whip until stiff and fold into chocolate-egg mixture:

6	**Egg whites***
1 pinch	**Cream of tartar**

Chill for 6 hours in refrigerator.

*Warning: Raw eggs may contain Salmonella.

Zabaglione Cassis

This is a treat, rich yet simple. I made it many years ago when we lived in New York but created a new flavor for Blue Heron. It is normally made with Marsala wine but I like Blackberry Cassis.

1. In a small bowl whisk until pale in color, about 3 minutes:

6		Egg yolks
4	Tbs	**Maple syrup** or **honey**
1	tsp	**Ginger** freshly grated
1	pinch	**Salt**

2. Add slowly until thick:

³/4	cup	**Cassis** (blackberry wine)

3. Pour into a double boiler over medium heat and whisk until thick and increased to twice its volume.

4. Let cool to room temperature.

5. Serve in tiny dishes with fresh berries or by itself.

   Garnish with: **Grated Orange rind** or **Fresh mint**

Pies

Two Delicious Pie Crusts

Marica is the pie crust maker in this family. She just whips them out. I often resort to buying them, but they don't taste nearly as good. These make enough for two bottom crusts, or a top and bottom.

Basic Pie Crust

1. In a medium bowl combine: (Use a knife to shave slices of butter into the flour mixture. Then with your fingers, rub butter into the flour mixture until it resembles sand-like granules.)

1½ cups	White flour
1 Tbs	Sugar
¼ tsp	Salt
8 Tbs	Butter (one stick)

2. Add water and then with your hands stir gently, making dough into a ball.

3 Tbs	Water

3. Divide into 2 balls. Roll out dough on floured wooden board.

4. Place flattened dough in a 9-inch buttered pie dish.

Bake at 350° for 10 minutes.

Whole Wheat Pie Crust

This is a nice variation to the recipe above.

Follow directions for **Basic Pie Crust** above.

1 cup	Whole wheat flour
½ cup	White flour
2 Tbs	Sugar
8 Tbs	Butter (one stick)
¼ tsp	Cinnamon
¼ tsp	Salt
2 Tbs	Water
1 Tbs	Lemon juice

Blue Heron Apple Pie

Serves 6

Our property is full of manzanita trees that bear little sour berries, whose taste has a slight resemblance to apples. The name means little apple. These unusual and graceful trees are slow growing. They are a very hard wood with a bark that is smooth and wine-colored. Each year the bark splits open and peels back to reveal a lime green trunk underneath. You can eat the peel of these little apples, but they do not satisfy our love for apples, so we planted forty different varieties on our property. We lost track of which ones are which, but we enjoy walking around and tasting the different apple flavors from the trees, whose apples ripen in late August. We pick an armload for Marica to make the best apple pies.

Preheat oven to 350°.

1. Pre-bake bottom half of the pie crust dough from page 152, and put aside the rest of the pie dough for the top of the pie.
   Bake at 350° for 10 minutes.

1 cup	**Water**
10	**Apples** peeled, cored, and sliced

Filling

2. Place the sliced apples in a large pot:
   Cook about 10 minutes.

3. Add to apples:

2 Tbs	**Butter** melted
1/4 cup	**Sugar** or **brown sugar**
1 Tbs	**Lemon juice**
1/2 tsp	**Cinnamon**
2 Tbs	**Kuzu*** or **corn starch** dissolved in 1/4 cup water

4. Pour filling into pie crust.

5. Roll out and arrange remaining dough to cover apples completely.

1 Tbs	**Sugar**
1/2	**Lemon** juiced

6. Sprinkle sugar and squeeze lemon juice evenly over top of pie crust. Cut a small x in the top of the crust to release steam while baking.

Bake at 350° for 30–40 minutes or until golden brown.

*Kuzu is a natural thickening agent that I prefer to use; you can buy it in any health food store.

Blueberry Peach Pie

.... *Makes one pie* ....

We eagerly anticipate our summer harvest of fresh peaches for this
seasonal pie.

Preheat oven to 350°.

1. Pre-bake bottom half of the pie crust
   dough from page 152, and put aside the rest
   of the pie dough for the top of the pie.

Bake at 350° for 10 minutes.

Filling

2. Slice and place in a bowl:

8		**Peaches** peeled and sliced
1	Tbs	**Butter** melted
¼	cup	**Raw** or **brown sugar**
⅛	tsp	**Nutmeg**
⅛	tsp	**Salt**
2	Tbs	**Kuzu** or **corn starch** dissolved in ¼ cup water

3. Pour pie filling into pie crust and
   add blueberries on top:

2	cups	**Fresh blueberries**

4. Roll out the remaining pie dough and
   place over pie. Pinch the top edges to
   the bottom crust. Cut a small x in the
   top to release steam while baking.

**Kuzu is a natural thickening agent
that I prefer to use; you can buy
it in any health food store.*

Bake at 350° for 35 minutes
or until golden.

Persian Mulberry Peach Pie

Makes one pie

This pie is great and so easy to make. We have wonderful peach trees on our property and an exceptional Persian mulberry tree. This combination is the best, but if you need to you can use blackberries in place of the mulberries.

Preheat oven to 350°.

1. Combine on bottom of a 9-inch buttered pie dish:

1¹/₂ cups	Granola
1 Tbs	Maple syrup

2. In a medium bowl blend:

1	Egg
1 Tbs	Maple syrup
³/₄ cup	Goat cheese
2 Tbs	Whole wheat flour
¹/₄ tsp	Nutmeg

3. Pour mixture over granola.

4. Add on top:

8	**Peaches** skinned and sliced

5. Place over peaches:

1 cup	**Mulberries** or **blackberries**

Bake at 350° for 30 minutes.

Genevieve's Lemon Meringue Pie

Serves 8

This recipe is inspired by Genevieve who was a wonderful cook. Her presence made a huge difference in my young life.

Preheat oven to 350°.

1. **Prebake crust** for **10 minutes.** Remove and turn oven down to 300°.

1	**Pie crust** on page 152; make ¹/₂ the recipe

2. In a medium bowl combine and mix together:

7	**Egg yolks** (save egg whites)
2 Tbs	**Corn starch** or **Kuzu***
¹/₂ cup	**Sugar**
³/₄ cup	**Water**
1 Tbs	**Lemon rind** grated or peeled
³/₄ cup	**Lemon juice**
8 Tbs	**Butter** cold and cut into chunks

3. Pour into a pot sitting in another pot with an inch of water, over medium heat. Stir constantly until thick, **10–12 minutes.**

4. Pour lemon mixture into pie crust.

5. Beat in separate bowl, until stiff:

4	**Egg whites**

6. Add to egg whites:

¹/₄ cup	**Sugar**

7. Spread evenly over pie, making little wave peaks with spoon.

Bake at 300° for 10 minutes.

*Kuzu is a natural thickening agent that I prefer to use; you can buy it in any health food store.

Mitzi's Chocolate Pecan Pie

.... *Serves 6* ....

Mitzi lived on our property for a year, and one of her great offerings was her Chocolate Pecan Pie. It is one of those desserts that is so great and so rich that you can't eat it often. It is a very special treat.

Preheat oven to 350°.

1. **Prebake for 10 minutes:**	1	**Pie crust** on page 152; make 1/2 the recipe
2. Place in the bottom of the pie crust:	3 oz	**Unsweetened dark chocolate** broken into chunks
3. In a medium pot combine and heat until melted:	4 oz 4 Tbs	**Unsweetened dark chocolate** **Butter**
4. Remove and add:	2 cups 1/4 cup 2 1 tsp 1/4 tsp 3 Tbs	**Brown sugar** or **raw sugar** **Milk** **Eggs** **Vanilla** **Salt** **Whole wheat flour**
5. Add:	3 cups	**Pecans** placed on top; gently push about 2/3 down into the chocolate mixture; the remaining 1/3 pecans should remain on top

Bake at 375° for 35–40 minutes.

If the pie crust starts to darken before 30 minutes, place aluminum foil over the pie and finish baking until pie is set.

Autumn Pumpkin Pie

Serves 10

Pumpkin pie is easy and festive for holidays. We always serve it for Thanksgiving. Here's my favorite. Pumpkins tend to vary in sweetness. This recipe calls for a minimal amount of sugar; increase if needed.

Preheat oven to 350°.

1. **Prebake for 10 minutes:**

2. Slice and steam until soft: When cooled, peel and puree.

3. In a large bowl combine and mix:

4. Combine pumpkin puree with the above mixture.

5. Fill pre-baked pie crusts evenly with pumpkin mixture.

   Bake at 425° for 10 minutes.

   Bake at 375° for another 45 minutes.

   Let cool before serving.

2		**Pie crusts** on page 152
2	2-lb	**Sugar pumpkins** (makes about 4 cups)
6		**Eggs**
¾ cup		**Sugar**
1 cup		**Milk** or **soy milk**
2 tsp		**Vanilla**
2 tsp		**Ginger** fresh, grated or minced
1 tsp		**Cinnamon**
1 pinch		**Cloves**
1 pinch		**Salt**
1		**Lemon rind** grated
4 drops		**Lemon extract**

Apple Crunch

·· *Serves 6* ··

This easy and foolproof recipe is a delight.

Preheat oven to 450°.

1. In a medium bowl combine:

3 cups	**Granola**
2 Tbs	**Butter** melted

2. In a small separate bowl combine:

¼ cup	**Sugar**
¼ tsp	**Nutmeg**
¼ tsp	**Cinnamon**

3. In a third bowl combine:

6 large	**Apples** peeled and sliced
2 Tbs	**Lemon juice**
2 Tbs	**Water**

4. Layer in a 9 x 13-inch buttered baking dish and cover with aluminum foil:

⅓ Granola
½ Sugar mixture
½ Apples
⅓ Granola
½ Sugar mixture
½ Apples
⅓ Granola

Bake covered at 450° for 35 minutes.

Bake uncovered at 350° for another **10 minutes.**

Living Off the Grid

It has been twenty-five years since we started clearing and began building on our forty acres of land. We slowly developed our property from a vast, dusty, overgrown sea of chaparral to a lush green oasis, populated with trees of every kind. We established a redwood grove inspired by an 1896 survey that used redwood trees on the site as markers, even though this isn't redwood country. We planted many varieties of pine—Italian, Indian, and Japanese— and we put in maple and *liquidambar*, which mimic the colors of fall in the East. We planted a variety of fruit and nut trees that have become too much for us to handle: apple, pear, cherry, plum, peach, apricot, mulberry, fig, almond, walnut, and many citrus. We have raspberries and blackberries, and we struggle with our two avocado trees that can't handle frost.

The temperatures here swing widely. In the winter we see temperatures as low as 18 to 20 degrees at night that can climb up to the 70s or 80s during the day. In the summer we go from 50 to 60 degrees at night up to 105 degrees or more in the late afternoon. And there is little or no rain from May to October.

We designed and sited buildings carefully to accommodate the weather. The building, laying of stonework, and landscaping was an evolutionary process that went on for years with minimal imposition, as far as possible, on the integrity of the land. Enrico would walk around, and walk around some more, then have me walk with him while he thought out loud, "You know, I've been consider-ing clearing the rocks in this area and adding a few mulberry or olive trees for a wind and fire break." Then another area would be cleared and planted with a different kind of tree that would feel very natural to and part of the native landscape. We undertook building projects according to our changing needs, putting in several separate buildings in addition to our house and workshop. Three structures now surround a simple, round, stone fountain: the main house, the Zendo (meditation house), and a dining house used when we host retreats and also as an overflow guest house.

Even though we are in the National Forest, living off the grid, we have managed to bring some comforts to our home. Our electricity comes from an elaborate solar-power system, which charges a huge battery pack. A generator supplements the solar panels during cloudy periods or days that have a heavy electrical load. I remember suggesting to Enrico that whatever number of panels we think we will need, he should double the number. In the end he tripled it, and still we never seem to have enough. We use propane for our refrigerators, clothes dryer, water heater, and kitchen stove, some of which are very recent acquisitions. We had no telephone for the first five years until we installed a radiophone, which consists of a receiver and transmitter at our house plus another set installed at a friend's over a mile away, where it connects to a regular telephone line. Our cell phones work if we connect them to an antenna on the roof. It is great for emergencies or when our regular line doesn't operate, which happens often enough.

It is interesting how easily we get along without all these conveniences when they're impossible to have, and yet how desperately we want them when we can get them. Today we have a satellite for our computers, although we do not have a television hookup, which we do not miss at all. I sometimes wonder if we have gone too far in bringing conveniences here. Nevertheless, the quietness and beauty of this wilderness is so pervasive that our technology seems not to infect the purity of the land. People who come here comment on the peacefulness and unusual energy that this land holds.

We often have family and friends visiting. Others come for one reason or another and in some cases end up living and working here. We have had our share of interesting characters, from young hippie enthusiasts who lived in a tent with goats and chickens to others who were more interested in Zen practice. We have had old and young, women and men, mostly single and usually in a life transition. It often creates a positive situation all around because we can always use their help and they are needing a break from their usual lives.

Other interesting visitors come from the animal world. Our property is surrounded by miles of National Forest and has a river flowing through that provides water for our orchards and trees. The trees, fruit, and water in turn provide shelter and food for the many creatures that live in the wild here. Bear are occasional visitors. One night I found one outside our window eating from the dog food bin. He kept returning even after the food was moved, and we had many close encounters, scaring him off with loud noises. A few years later another bear entered one of our guest trailers and ate all the flour he found in the cupboard.

He never returned, perhaps due to a sick stomach. Mountain lions are around. I have not seen any but have heard them on numerous occasions.

Apparently people who are hiking have some concern about them, but we have not had any problems so far. Bobcats have eaten our chickens, and one Christmas we had to catch one and drive him far over the mountains, about fifteen miles away, so he wouldn't return. Rattlesnakes are everywhere, and watching out for them becomes second nature. We taught the children to keep their eyes open, and so far the only bites have happened when two of our dogs got bitten in the face when they tried to play with the snakes.

We live only ninety miles north of Los Angeles and yet it feels as though we are in another world out here. Our thirty-minute drive to Ojai feels much longer, because it is as though you have to go through a compression to shift into the bustling world. Nevertheless, Ojai is the perfect town to live near. It is an artistic and spiritually based community that is wonderful for raising children. Many children come back to live here when they are grown. Our children are living in the area. One daughter lives on our land and is married with two children; she has opened her own ballet school and is doing well. Our other daughter is nearby with three little children. All five grandchildren love it here, as did our kids when they were young.

Cookies

Cardamom Cookies

·············· *Makes 20 cookies* ··············

These are wonderful and healthy cookies.

Preheat oven to 350°.

1. In a large bowl mix together:

2	**Eggs**
¼ cup	**Milk**
8 Tbs	**Butter** melted
¾ cup	**Honey**
2 Tbs	**Orange rind** grated
2 tsp	**Cardamom**
½ tsp	**Ginger**
1 pinch	**Cloves**

2. Add:

4 cups	**Whole wheat flour**
1 tsp	**Baking powder**

3. Spoon onto a buttered cookie sheet and press down to flatten.

   Bake at 350° for 8–10 minutes
   or until golden brown.
   Larger cookies may need more baking time.

   Optional:
   Add **⅓ cup carob chips**
   or **chocolate chips** to dough
   before baking.

Blue Heron Chocolate Chip Cookies

·························· *Makes 24 cookies* ··························

These are my favorite cookies. My very favorite. You can't get any better.

Preheat oven to 350°.

1. Mix together in this order:

3	**Eggs**
1 cup	**Raw sugar**
1 cup	**Butter** melted (2 sticks)
1 tsp	**Vanilla**
1	**Lemon rind** grated
¼ tsp	**Salt**

2. Add in order given and stir in as you go along:

   Add flour, baking soda, and baking powder all together before stirring in.

3 cups	**Rolled oats**
½ cup	**Coconut** shredded
1 cup	**Chocolate chips** bittersweet
2½ cups	**Whole wheat flour**
1 tsp	**Baking soda**
½ tsp	**Baking powder**

3. Spoon loosely into balls on buttered cookie sheet. Do not squeeze batter when making each cookie.

   Bake at 350° for 20 minutes or until browned.

Genevieve's Butter Walnut Cookies

Makes 20 cookies

These were my mother's favorite cookies. I have special memories of my mother enjoying her cookies and ice cream. These were at the top of her list. Genevieve used to make them, and we always waited until they just got out of the oven. They are very thin and crispy. When warm, they are outrageous.

Preheat oven to 300°.

1. In a large bowl mix together:

8 Tbs	**Butter** melted (one stick)
1	**Egg**
1 cup	**Brown sugar**
1 tsp	**Almond extract**
1 tsp	**Vanilla**
1 pinch	**Salt**

2. Add:

1/2 cup	**White flour**
1 tsp	**Baking powder**
2 cups	**Whole walnuts**

3. Put aluminum foil on cookie sheet and butter it.
   Spoon less than 1 tsp for each cookie; they spread a lot.

Bake at 300° for 15 minutes or until browned.

Tip: Can be wonderful broken into pieces over ice cream

Cakes

Aunt Ev's Cardamom Bundt Cake

Serves 8

Enrico's Aunt Ev always made bundt cakes and it inspired Marica to try them. They are wonderful.

Preheat oven to 325°.

1. In a large bowl mix together:

8 Tbs	**Butter** melted (one stick)
1 cup	**Raw sugar**
3	**Eggs**
1 tsp	**Vanilla**

2. Add to wet ingredients:

2 cups	**White flour**
1 Tbs	**Cardamom** ground
1/4 tsp	**Cinnamon** ground
1/4 tsp	**Nutmeg** ground
1 Tbs	**Orange rind** grated
2 tsp	**Baking powder**
1/4 tsp	**Salt**

3. Add to batter and mix all together:

1 cup	**Sour cream** or **yogurt**

4. Butter and dust with flour a 10-inch bundt pan. Pour mixture into the pan.

Bake at 325° for 45–50 minutes
or until a thin knife inserted into cake comes out clean.

Lemon Cranberry Bundt Cake

.... *Serves 6* ....

This is a great way to use up extra cranberries during the holidays.

Preheat oven to 350°.

1. In a large bowl mix together:

3	**Eggs**
³/₄ cup	**Butter** melted (1¹/₂ sticks)
¹/₂ cup	**Honey**
1 Tbs	**Lemon rind** grated
1 cup	**Cranberries**

2. Pour on top of above mixture, and mix together:

1¹/₂ cups	**Whole wheat flour**
³/₄ tsp	**Baking powder**
¹/₄ tsp	**Salt**

In a 10-inch buttered bundt pan **bake at 350° for 45 minutes** or until a thin knife inserted into cake comes out clean.

Wait until cake has cooled before you turn it over.

Icing

In a small bowl whisk or beat:

2 Tbs	**Butter** melted
1 Tbs	**Water**
¹/₂ cup	**Powdered sugar**
1 Tbs	**Lemon rind** grated fine

Drip over the top of cake.

Chocolate Marble Bundt Cake

Serves 8

Marica used to make this cake a lot for her husband and their friend Brent when they all lived in a house in Ojai. If you don't have a bundt pan you can use two bread pans.

Preheat oven to 350°.

1. In a large bowl mix together:

3	Eggs
8 Tbs	**Butter** melted (one stick)
1 cup	Milk
1/2 cup	Yogurt
2 tsp	Vanilla
2/3 cup	Sugar

2. Add and mix:

4 cups	**White** or **whole wheat flour**
2 1/2 tsp	**Baking powder**
1/8 tsp	**Salt**

3. In a small bowl mix well until it resembles chocolate sauce:

1/2 cup	**Cocoa powder** unsweetened
1/3 cup	**Sugar**
1/2 cup	**Rum** or milk

4. In a separate bowl crumble with fingers until mixture resembles coarse crumbs:

1/2 cup	**Flour**
4 Tbs	**Butter** cold, cut into small pieces
1/4 cup	**Sugar**
1 tsp	**Cinnamon**
1 tsp	**Nutmeg**
1 tsp	**Cardamom**

5. Sprinkle 1/2 crumble in the bottom of a buttered 10-inch bundt or two bread pans. Pour in batter. Sprinkle the rest of crumble on top.

   Bake at 350° for 50–60 minutes or until a thin knife inserted into cake comes out clean.

Chocolate Apple Sauce Cake

This makes a great layered cake. The following recipe makes two layers.

Preheat oven to 350°.

1. In a large bowl mix together:

8 Tbs	**Butter** melted (one stick)
4	**Eggs**
1 cup	**Apple sauce**
1¼ cups	**Raw sugar** or **brown sugar**
⅔ cup	**Milk** or **soy milk**
⅔ cup	**Yogurt**
1 tsp	**Vanilla**

2. In a separate bowl mix:

1 cup	**White flour**
1 cup	**Whole wheat flour**
1 tsp	**Baking powder**
1 tsp	**Baking soda**
1 cup	**Cocoa** unsweetened or **carob powder** (or ⅓ cup of each)
¼ tsp	**Salt**

3. Pour into two 9-inch round buttered baking dishes.

   Bake at 350° for 30 minutes or until a thin knife inserted into cake comes out clean.

Icing

In a small pan melt and mix together:

1 cup	**Dark chocolate chips**
¼ cup	**Sugar**
4 Tbs	**Butter**
1 tsp	**Vanilla**
1 pinch	**Salt**

Let cake cool.

To layer cake spread ½ of the icing between both layers. With remaining icing cover the top, letting it drip down the sides.

Birthday Coconut Cake

When I was a little girl I always asked for a coconut cake for my birthday. I never got the recipe for it but I made up my own, and it is definitely more healthy and really tasty. It is my favorite. Sometimes my kids offer to make it for me on my birthday.

Preheat oven to 350°.

1. In a large bowl mix together:

4	**Eggs**
4 Tbs	**Butter** melted
14 oz	**Coconut milk**
3/4 cup	**Raw sugar**
1 1/2 tsp	**Vanilla**
1 1/2 Tbs	**Lemon rind** grated

2. Add by pouring all the following ingredients over the above mixture, and then stir:

2 cups	**Whole wheat flour**
1 cup	**Coconut**
1 1/2 tsp	**Baking powder**
1 pinch	**Cardamom**
1/4 tsp	**Salt**

3. Place all over the top of cake:

1 8-oz can	**Pineapple chunks**

4. Pour into a buttered bundt pan or 9 x 9-inch baking dish.

   Bake at 350° for 40 minutes or until a thin knife inserted into cake comes out clean.

Optional icing instead of pineapple chunks

1. In a medium bowl combine:

3/4 cup	**Butter** melted (1 1/2 sticks)
3/4 cup	**Sugar** raw
1 1/2 tsp	**Vanilla**
1 1/4 cups	**Coconut** shredded

2. When cake has cooled, spread on icing.

3. Heat under broiler for a few minutes until browned.

Persian Mulberry Cake
with Goat Cheese

.... *Serves 6* ....

This is an unusual cake with goat cheese and mulberries. I highly recommend it.

Preheat oven to 350°.

1. In a large bowl mix together:

4		**Eggs**
8 Tbs		**Butter** melted (one stick)
1 cup		**Milk** or **soy milk**
1/2 cup		Raw sugar
1/4 cup		**Goat cheese**
1 Tbs		**Lemon** grated rind

2. Pour on top of egg mixture and mix in:

2 cups		**Whole wheat flour**
1 tsp		**Baking powder**

3. Add and stir in gently:

4 cups		**Mulberries** or **blackberries**

4. Pour into buttered 9 x 9-inch baking dish, or two buttered bread pans.

   Bake at 350° for 45 minutes
   or until a thin knife inserted into cake comes out clean.

June Apricot Cake

Serves 6

In June, Ojai is filled with apricots.

Preheat oven to 350°.

1. Pour into a buttered 9 x 9-inch baking dish:

4 cups	**Apricots** fresh, cut into large pieces

2. Mix together and sprinkle over apricots:

2 Tbs	**Brown sugar**
1 Tbs	**Lemon juice**

3. In a medium bowl mix:

1/3 cup	**Raw sugar**
1/3 cup	**Molasses**
1	**Egg**
4 Tbs	**Butter** melted
1/2 cup	**Yogurt** or **soy milk**

4. In a large bowl mix:

1 1/2 cups	**Whole wheat flour**
2 tsp	**Baking powder**
1/2 tsp	**Baking soda**
1 tsp	**Ground ginger**
1/4 tsp	**Nutmeg**

5. Combine wet and dry ingredients.

6. Pour batter over apricots in baking dish.

   Bake at 350° for 45 minutes or until a thin knife inserted into cake comes out clean.

Pear Upside-Down Cake

Serves 6

This is a wonderful treat for an afternoon tea.

Preheat oven to 350°.

1. In a buttered 9 x 9-inch baking dish place:

4 fresh	**Pears** or **apples** peeled and cut into large pieces

2. Sprinkle over pears:

2 Tbs	**Brown sugar**
1 tsp	**Lemon juice**
¼ tsp	**Nutmeg**
1 Tbs	**Flour**

3. In a large bowl mix together:

2	**Eggs**
8 Tbs	**Butter** softened (one stick)
½ cup	**Milk** or **soy milk**
1 tsp	**Vanilla**
¼ tsp	**Almond extract**

4. Mix together into a crumble, then add egg to mixture and mix more:

2 cups	**White flour**
2 tsp	**Baking powder**
⅓ cup	**Sugar**
½ tsp	**Cinnamon**
¼ tsp	**Nutmeg**
1 pinch	**Salt**
1	**Lemon rind** grated

5. Press mixture on top of pears until completely covered.

Bake at 350° for 40 minutes or until cake moves away from the sides of pan.

Meyer Lemon Half-Pound Cake

In our orchard we grow Meyer lemon trees, which are a mixture of orange and lemon. This fruit looks and tastes like lemon but is a little warmer in color and tastes a little sweeter. We use these lemons interchangeably with the typical ones and love them.

Preheat oven to 350°.

1. In a large bowl mix:

8 Tbs	**Butter** softened (one stick)
3/4 cup	**Raw Sugar**
3	**Eggs** mix in one at a time
1/2 tsp	**Lemon extract**
1/2 tsp	**Vanilla extract**

2. Add to egg mixture and mix in:

2 1/4 cups	**White flour**
1 tsp	**Baking powder**
1 pinch	**Salt**

3. Add and mix into batter:

1/2 cup	**Milk** or **soy milk**
1/4 cup	**Yogurt**

4. Add and mix in:

1/4 cup	**Lemon** juice
1 Tbs	**Lemon rind** grated

5. Butter a bread pan and dust with flour.

   Bake at 350° for 60–80 minutes
   or until a thin knife inserted into cake comes out clean.

Carob Coconut Brownies

Serves 6

For those who want to avoid chocolate yet love brownies, these are great.
And for those who love chocolate, these are still a real treat.

Preheat oven to 350°.

1. In a large bowl mix:

6 Tbs	**Butter** melted
1/3 cup	**Honey**
2	**Eggs**
2 Tbs	**Orange rind** grated
2 Tbs	**Water**

2. In a separate bowl combine:

1 cup	**Whole wheat flour**
1/2 cup	**Carob powder** or **cocoa**
1/2 tsp	**Baking soda**
1/2 cup	**Coconut**
1 pinch	**Salt**

3. Combine wet and dry ingredients and pour into a buttered 9 x 9-inch square baking dish.

   Bake at 350° for 25–30 minutes or until a thin knife inserted into brownies comes out clean.

Tiramochamisu or Tiramintmisu Cake

Serves 8–10

Tiramochamisu Cake is usually a favorite. Try the mint for a great variation.

1. Brew and set aside:

   1 cup   Coffee or **mint tea** strong

2. In a large bowl beat until stiff:

   4 cups   Cream heavy

3. Add and mix in cream.

   8 Tbs   Sweet cocoa powder
   2 tsp   Vanilla
   2 tsp   Coffee ground fine
   (if making mint do not add)

4. In a separate bowl grate:
   (This dish is layered, so use half the ingredients for each layer.)

   1 oz   Unsweetened chocolate

5. Dip one at a time into coffee or mint tea for a split second and place 18 of the 36 lady fingers in the bottom of a 9 x 9-inch baking dish.

   36   Lady fingers
   (buy at any grocery store)

6. Spread 1/2 cream mixture over the top of the lady fingers.

   Optional: Spread a layer of raspberries on top of the first cream layer in step 6.

7. Sprinkle 1/2 grated chocolate evenly on top of cream.

8. Repeat layering. Cover with plastic wrap and refrigerate for a few hours.

Vincenzo and Kana's Wedding Cake

Marica offered to make the wedding cake for Vincenzo and Kana's wedding. The following is enough for only eight people. The eventual wedding cake was for a hundred people.

Preheat oven to 350°.

1. Sift into large bowl:

2²/3 cups	White flour
2¹/4 tsp	Baking powder
¹/2 tsp	Salt

2. In a large bowl whisk butter with electric whisk until creamy then add vanilla and lemon extract:

1 cup	Butter softened (2 sticks)
1¹/2 tsp	Vanilla
¹/2 tsp	Lemon extract

3. Add and continue to whisk:

1 cup	Sugar

4. Add all at one time:

4 large	Egg yolks (save whites in separate bowl)

5. Add ¹/3 amount of milk to batter, then add ¹/3 flour mixture. Continue adding milk and flour, alternating until all three mixtures are in one bowl.

1 cup	Milk

6. Whisk until stiff and fold into batter:

4	Egg whites

Bake at 350° for 25–30 minutes
in two 9-inch buttered round cake pans.

*For icing and filling between layers,
see page 187.*

Wedding Cake Filling and Icing

Filling between layers

1. In a double boiler combine and mix together:

4	Egg yolks
4 tsp	Corn starch or **Kuzu***
1/3 cup	Sugar
1/3 cup	Water
2 tsp	Lemon grated rind
1/3 cup	Lemon juice
4 Tbs	Butter cold and cut into chunks

2. Stir constantly over medium heat until thick, **10–12 minutes.**

*Kuzu is a natural thickening agent that I prefer to use; you can buy it in any health food store.

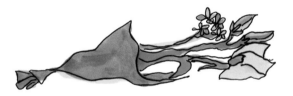

Icing to be poured over top

1. In a medium bowl cream together until smooth:

4 Tbs	Butter room temperature
1 cup	Cream cheese whipped
1/2 cup	Sugar

2. Add while still beating:

1/3 cup	Yogurt
2 tsp	Vanilla
1 pinch	Salt

Decorate cake with edible flowers

Our Zen Center

Over the last twenty-five years, Enrico has been to many Zen retreats. The first was in New York at the Rochester Zen Center when Philip Kapleau, the Zen teacher, was still there. I remember Enrico complaining about the questionnaire he had to fill out to prove he was capable of doing the three-week training. He found the retreat valuable even though the level of intensity wasn't difficult. However, when we moved to California, Enrico decided to try a seven-day retreat, at Mt. Baldy Zen Center. Mt. Baldy is considered the most rigorous Zen center in the country, yet it required no questionnaire. Anyone can go, even if you have no experience. Some people have found themselves there by chance, not realizing what they were in for. On a typical day you get up at 3:00 in the morning to sit and chant, and you see the Zen master privately four times a day. And you sit and sit and sit, sometimes through the night.

I thought Enrico was insane to go, and I told him I could never consider doing a retreat there or anywhere. However, Enrico did these seven-day retreats, called sesshins, at least a couple of times a year. At home he likes to sit one to two hours each morning in the beautiful little tea house we built. He used to often suggest that I sit, that it was very important to experience the self from a nonthinking place. I told him I had my own way of working and that sitting wasn't my thing.

A few years later a friend recommended Jikoji, another Zen center, up north near Santa Cruz. Enrico, trusting this friend, decided to go.

There are two branches of Zen: Rinzi and Soto. They each have a different approach. Rinzi is much harsher and immediate; Soto, softer and more gradual. Mt. Baldy was typical Rinzi, and Jikoji was Soto. Enrico had realized by now that he preferred Soto, and one day when Enrico was signing up for another retreat at Jikoji, I said I would go too—God knows why! I had never sat and suddenly I was ready to go do a sesshin? Enrico gave me quick instructions on how to sit. He said your posture is very important. He explained Orioki, an elaborate ritual around meals that includes the way you handle your set of bowls during meals while chanting. He described the schedule of sittings and talks given by the teacher and how once a day you do Dokusan, which is a private meeting with the Roshi.

The only question was, what to do with the kids? We had never left them with anyone for more than a couple of hours. But when Enrico called Jikoji, they told us we could bring the whole family. That was it! I was delighted. We brought all our camping gear: tents, ice chests, sleeping bags, and so on. We decided to split the week: Enrico would do the first half while I took care of the children, and I, the last three days.

Kobun, the Zen master, was wonderful with our children. I was impressed. I really liked Kobun and liked the fact that when he and I had our private meeting he told me how he didn't like doing Dokusan. He also didn't like giving talks in the evening. His honesty, his depth and sensitivity were significant to me. He was very human and also profound. Perhaps it allowed me to see that this work isn't about being superhuman but just learning to do the best you can, and suddenly it all felt more available to me. I was really pleasantly surprised.

I also found I could sit. I had been very nervous about that part of it, but when the time came I handled it. To get through that first time, I felt I cheated because I used fantasy: made plans, had conversations with people in my imagination, imagined I was dancing, anything. I am sure that the presence of all the other people sitting supported me.

I learned that sitting is an opportunity to watch yourself while in a dilemma. It is very clean. It took a while to learn not to judge my mental antics. I discovered another part of me that is almost impossible to find under the usual noise of everyday life. There is a larger me who can include all the various aspects of my ordinary self. This discovery is not a one-time thing, nor is it the same each time. It changes and develops as long as I give it the space and attention it needs.

By the end of my few days I was so "up" that I said to Enrico, "Let's start our own Zen center." I had sat only three-and-a-half days and now I had this absurd idea. But Enrico was delighted. He admitted he wanted to do something like that for years but would have never considered it without my equal enthusiasm. So I ran up to Kobun at the end of the sesshin and told him of my idea. Much to my surprise he seemed very pleased, and told us he would even come down when we were ready to hold our first sesshin. I was thrilled. We already had built a little Zendo, a place to sit, the year before. The dining house was not complete when we had our first weekend sesshin in April 1990. Kobun came down to help with the opening with a few people from his center. Some of our friends and family came as well. Enrico and I worked out a very simple schedule that included only some of the usual rituals. We maintained silence and announced everything by bells. We had a discussion group each morning, in place of the talks and private sessions.

I cooked the meals with help from different participants. We had our meals in the unfinished dining house, sitting on homemade buckwheat pillows on the floor around low tables. We each had our own set of bowls and ate in silence without elaborate rituals. That first sesshin the sun beat down on our heads at lunch and the cool winds of evening chilled our bones, but we managed. The whole weekend was very special and our Zen center was met with enthusiasm.

For many years we offered sesshins one weekend a month, plus two eight-day retreats each year.

But very recently we have reduced the number because we have been giving other workshops here.

Our Zen center is small. We can accommodate only eight to ten people at a time. At first I felt we should be bigger—that smaller meant we weren't a real Zen center. But as the years have gone by we have developed a wonderful group of people who have been really committed. We have all evolved together, and I feel that this has been valuable. I soon learned that the number of participants doesn't signify anything.

In the last few years the flavor of our sesshins has changed too. We still sit as before and have the same schedule, but something more is included these days, a softer attitude maybe—a deeper and broader understanding of what interferes with the beauty of just being.

Sauces

Ginger Honey Sauce

This sauce is easy, very tasty, and you may have all the ingredients on hand. It is especially good over rice dishes with vegetables.

In a small saucepan combine and heat but do not boil:

Serve over:
Tofu
Fish
Chicken

1 cup	**Water**
1/2 cup	**Tamari**
1 Tbs	**Rice vinegar**
2 1/2 Tbs	**Honey**
2 tsp	**Ginger** fresh, grated

Matilija Tamari Sauce

This recipe has a few more ingredients and is a little more intense than Ginger Honey Sauce.

In a small saucepan combine and heat but do not boil:

2/3 cup	**Water**
1/2 cup	**Tamari**
2 Tbs	**Rice vinegar**
2 Tbs	**Honey**
1 tsp	**Ginger** grated
1 clove	**Garlic** minced
1 Tbs	**Mirin** or **sherry**
3	**Green onions** chopped

Serve over rice, vegetables, chicken, or fish.

Ojai Lemon Sauce

This is great over fish. Either braise the fish or bake it with the following ingredients.

In a small pot heat until butter is melted:

8 Tbs	**Butter** unsalted (one stick)
1/2	**Lemon** juiced
4 cloves	**Garlic** minced
1/4 cup	**White wine**

Green Enchilada Sauce

Serves 6

This sauce is wonderful with Black Bean Enchiladas on page 33.

1. Roast on a dry pan for 20 minutes at 450°.

    Let cool, peel, and remove seeds.

    8 fresh   **Anaheim chilies**

2. Chop and saute in a large pan:

    2 Tbs   **Olive oil**
    2   **Red onions** diced
    4 cloves   **Garlic** minced
    1 fresh   **Jalapeno pepper** diced
    12   **Tomatillos** peeled and diced
    ¼ cup   **Cilantro**
       Salt and **pepper** to taste

3. Blend in a blender all of the above ingredients, until they are a textured soup consistency.

Pesto Lemon Sauce

My sister-in-law Elaine introduced me to pesto and she uses it for many dishes. It has an unusual taste that is rich and refreshing at the same time.

1. In a blender combine:

1½ cups	**Basil** fresh
½ cup	**Cashews**

2. Slowly add:

1 cup	**Olive oil**
1 Tbs	**Lemon** juice
2 cloves	**Garlic**
½ cup	**Parmesan cheese**
	Salt and **pepper** to taste
½	**Cheddar Cheddar** grated

Suggestion:
Use on **Spaghetti**
　　　　Pizza
　　　　Vegetables
　　　　Tofu
　　　　Sandwiches

Mushroom Garlic Sauce

.... *Serves 4* ....

This is especially good over chicken or vegetables.

1. In a medium pot saute for
   5 minutes over a low flame:

1 Tbs	**Butter**
2	**Onions** sliced thin

2. Add and stir occasionally
   until thickened:

½ lb	**Mushrooms**
3 cloves	**Garlic** minced
2 cups	**Milk** or **soy milk**
3 Tbs	**Whole wheat flour**
	Salt and **pepper** to taste

Marinated Ginger

.... *Serves 6* ....

This recipe is from our friend Manouch who has been coming to our Zen retreats.

1. In a small pot bring to boil:

   | 12 oz | Rice vinegar |

2. Add and cook for 2 minutes on medium heat:

1 lb	**Ginger root** peeled and sliced thin
2 Tbs	**Salt**
1 Tbs	**Sugar**

3. Add:

   | ½ cup | **Lemon** juice |

4. Allow to cool before storing in a jar.

   Let marinate for a few days in the refrigerator.

Desert Hummus Sauce

.... *Serves 6* ....

We use hummus over beans and rice all the time. It is also a great addition to sandwiches or used as a dip with chips or vegetables. The recipe's simple, and fresh hummus is always a treat.

1. In a blender mix:

3 cups	**Chick peas** precooked
3/4 cup	**Tahini**
6 cloves	**Garlic** minced
1 large	**Lemon** juiced
	Salt and **pepper** to taste

2. Then add very slowly while blender is on a low speed:

1/2 cup	**Olive oil**

3. Sprinkle with:

	Paprika (do not stir in)

Festive Cranberry Sauce

Serves 6

This cranberry sauce is our very favorite for Thanksgiving.

1. In a medium pot combine:

8 cups	**Cranberries** fresh, rinsed and picked over
1 can	**Orange juice** 12 oz frozen, undiluted
1 cup	**Honey**
¼ tsp	**Cinnamon**

2. Bring cranberries to a boil and turn down the heat.
   Simmer for 10 minutes.

3. Let cool and refrigerate before serving.

Frankie's Hot Fudge on Ice Cream

Serves 6

I love a great hot fudge sundae. We sometimes make this for a birthday treat. The quality of the chocolate and ice cream is very important! Use dark chocolate and get the best ice cream you can find.

In a saucepan over low heat stir until melted (do not overheat):

8 oz	**Dark chocolate** or **semisweet chips**
¼ cup	**Milk** or **soy milk**
½ tsp	**Vanilla**

Serve over your favorite ice cream with sliced **bananas** *on top.*

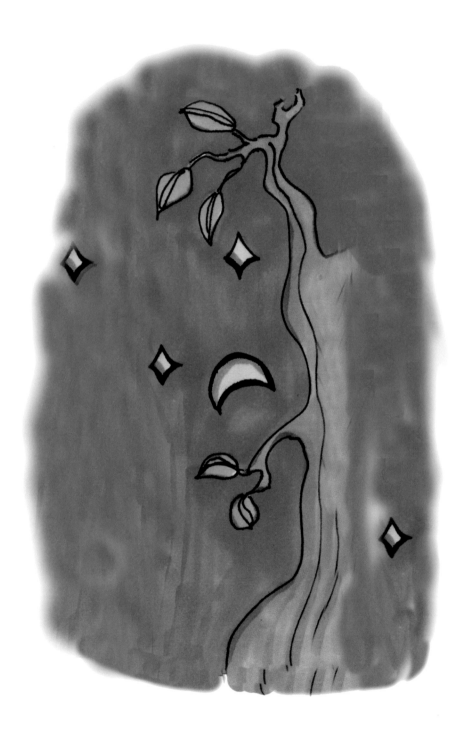

Drinks

Robin's Chai

Serves 6

When we first were here, a mysterious young couple plus two young brothers arrived on foot. They asked if they could live on our property in exchange for working one day of the week each week. With our okay they moved their teepees to the other side of our river. At that time their presence here was very supportive and helpful. We saw how beautiful their teepee was, and decided to buy and live in one while our house was being built. Every so often we got together for meals and they made this wonderful Chai. Then two years later they mysteriously disappeared, but this delicious recipe and our wonderful memories endure.

1. In a medium pot combine and simmer for 10 minutes:

6	cups	**Water**
3	inches	**Ginger root** cut in chunks
2	Tbs	**Cardamom seeds** whole peel off shell, grind slightly
2	sticks	**Cinnamon**
8		**Cloves**
8		**Peppercorns**

2. Add and let brew for 5 minutes then strain liquid through sieve and discard spices:

3		**Black tea bags** or favorite tea

3. Add and reheat slightly:

1	cup	**Milk** or **soy milk**
1	Tbs	**Honey** to taste (optional)

◄← THE BLUE HERON RANCH COOKBOOK

Teepee Hot Cider

.... *Serves 6* ....

This drink is wonderful on a cold winter night. Even here in sunny California we get below freezing temperatures and occasionally it will snow. When we lived in the teepee, we drank a lot of hot cider in the winter months.

1. In a large saucepan combine and heat:

4	cups	**Apple juice**
4	cups	**Cranberry juice**
2	Tbs	**Lemon juice**
1	stick	**Cinnamon**
1/8	tsp	**Cardamom seeds** whole peel off shell, grind slightly
1/2	tsp	**Cloves** whole
1	pinch	**Black pepper** to taste

2. Serve hot in mugs with:

1		**Orange** sliced thin floating on top

4th of July Lemonade

Serves 10

Sometimes we go out and pick a large bag of Meyer lemons and blood oranges for this drink. The blood oranges create a fabulous color. You can use regular lemons and oranges if these are not available.

1. Squeeze juice from:

18	**Lemons** Meyer lemons if possible
6	**Oranges**

2. Heat in a small pan and let steep until strong and cool:

2 cups	**Water**
½ cup	**Mint** fresh

3. Heat water in another small pan to dilute sugar and let cool:

2 cups	**Raw sugar**
2 cups	**Water**

4. Mix all together with ice and pour into two large pitchers:

2 trays	**Ice cubes** (about 8 cups of ice)

5. Add to each pitcher:

1 cup	**Mint** (½ cup to each pitcher)

Keep refrigerated until ready to serve.

If too concentrated, add more water to desired taste.

Christine's Punch

This punch was given to me by a fabulous cook, who is also my daughter's wonderful mother-in-law. She has been a chef at the world-renowned Ranch House restaurant in Ojai for many years and has generously offered this incredible punch.

1. In a medium pot boil:

   6 cups   **Water**

2. Add and steep for 15 minutes, then pour into very large bowl:

   16 bags   **Red Zinger tea**
   Celestial Seasons or any tea with hibiscus and/or orange blend

3. Add to tea:

   1 gallon   **Apple juice** unfiltered
   1 12-oz   **Frozen cranberry juice** (do not dilute)

4. Slice very thin to float on top of punch:

   1   **Orange** sliced thin

Honey Almond Chai

Serves 6

This healthy drink was created by Justin, Marica's husband. It is rich and creamy yet has no dairy products.

1. Steep tea:	**2**	**Chai** tea bags
	1¹/2 cups	**Water** boiling
2. In a large frying pan stir constantly over medium heat until coconut is browned:	**3/4 cup**	**Almonds**
	3/4 cup	**Cashews**
	3/4 cup	**Coconut**
3. In a blender combine nuts with the following ingredients and blend until smooth:	**1¹/2 cups**	**Soy milk** or **rice milk**
	1 tsp	**Vanilla**
	1/2 tsp	**Cinnamon powder**
	2 Tbs	**Honey** or **maple syrup**

4. Add chai tea and continue to blend.

Served chilled as a thick drink.

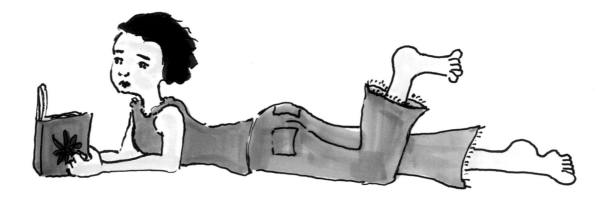

In Remembrance of Andrei

Andrei was the youngest of our children and like the others started drawing when he was very young. He particularly enjoyed drawing airplanes and vehicles, and hardly a day went by that he didn't spend at least part of it drawing. If he forgot to take his drawing pad when he went with us to a restaurant in town, he would ask for a napkin to draw on and would often leave it with a charming little message for the waiter or cook.

When Andrei was six years old, he spent a good amount of time hanging around my ballet studio watching his sisters dance, but soon enough he found his own interest, tennis. We were fortunate enough to find a really good teacher and over the years he developed into a beautiful and graceful player, but not a competitive one. He won awards for good sportsmanship and claimed he didn't mind not winning tournaments; he said he enjoyed playing so much it didn't matter. Andrei also took up fencing and again his grace and ease of movement helped him develop the skills easily.

When Andrei was twelve years old, he met a friend of ours in Ojai who is a shaman. Andrei was very clear that he wanted to learn the shaman's way and asked us if he could study under this man. This work became very important to Andrei and influenced his outlook on life for the next eight years.

During his teenage years, Andrei grew into a tall, lovely young man who found high school confusing. He would come home in the evenings and say that he was becoming two people, one at school and one at home. He couldn't figure out which one he should be because the one at school required a different personality, one that he didn't like, but the one at home wasn't adequate for the world at large.

At sixteen, Andrei discovered Tom Brown, a famous tracker and teacher. When Tom Brown was eight years old, he met and began studying with Stalking Wolf, an extraordinary Apache Indian scout and shaman. Later Tom started a school in Pine Barrens in New Jersey. There Andrei attended a series of week-long intensive trainings, each time returning more inspired. He often suggested that we too should go and study with Tom.

In the spring of Andrei's junior year of high school, his brother Vincenzo asked Andrei to assist him in a movie he was making in Toronto. We strongly encouraged him to go. He was there for five months working as his brother's personal assistant, making storyboards, and he even designed a weapon that was used in the film.

He returned home with little appetite for school but started painting quite seriously. The next year he attended Prescott College, majoring in art, but he did not return the following year. Andrei saw the world in a different way from most people, given his upbringing and shaman inclinations, and found it was a challenge for him to integrate into the so-called real world. He struggled with both trying to become part of the world and fighting for a deeper purpose that is not often acknowledged or appreciated.

Both our daughters had their share of problems integrating two worlds, ours and the world at large. Francesca went to Russia to study theater and dance, and there she met a Russian man and got married. Marica also married, though her husband is from Ojai. Both girls started families and are now raising children nearby.

In early January 2005, Enrico and I were away in Santa Barbara, he attending a retreat, and I, my graduate school program. Andrei was at home with Francesca, her husband Dmitry, and their two children.

It had been raining hard for more than a week. We had put up ropes to help us cross the swollen river on foot. Dmitry and Andrei were sitting by the fire talking, and Dmitry mentioned that Russians celebrated Christmas on that day, January 7. Andrei started talking about our Christmas and St. Nicholas and good and bad spirits. He said that in his view evil spirits were really good spirits who had accumulated evil, and he saw that his role in life was to take on that burden of evil. Dmitry replied that such a task is not for human endeavor, but Andrei said he would take it on anyway.

The following day Andrei received a call from a friend who drove some distance to Ojai to meet him on the other side of the river. Andrei held his intention to meet his friend even though the rain had intensified, and by that evening the river was raging as Andrei attempted to cross, and in so doing lost his life. The river claimed him. There isn't much more I want to say about that night except that for weeks the rain came down and it still hasn't stopped inside of me.

Andrei had a beautiful life here and he loved this place more than anyone. He spent many hours sitting, walking, and sensing the deep rhythms of this land, and now as I write this I feel his presence.

Raising a family in the somewhat unconventional way that we have has been both wonderful and heartbreaking, beyond anything I could have imagined. I realize now that there is no one "right" way. One has to do it the best one can. I have no regrets. I see now that we made some mistakes and I am perhaps blind to others. But what we did do, creating an oasis of love and calm, has been beautiful and that can never be taken away from any of us, especially Andrei.

I never understood community until this happened. The rains had closed all the roads into Ojai, and we were stranded in Santa Barbara for three days. Then we were stuck in Ojai for weeks until the road to Matilija Canyon was opened and the river dropped enough to cross on foot. It was during this time that people showed up in exquisite ways. I was overwhelmed by what our friends, and even people we didn't know, did for us. Houses were opened to us, rooms donated to us by hotels. Restaurants sent food. Friends carried in steaming platters of delicious food. The endless tasks and phone calls necessitated by such an event were taken on by other family members and close friends. Ojai, a town full of wonderful people, took us in and cared for us, and I thank you all with a gratitude that is beyond any words.

ANDREI NATALI & DIG 2005

Index

About the Author

Nadia Natali lives with her husband Enrico, a serious Zen practitioner and photographer, on Blue Heron Ranch high in the Matilija Canyon above Ojai, California. She and Enrico host numerous weekend and eight-day retreats at the ranch. Nadia cooks all the meals as well as participating in the meditations.

Raised in Westport, Connecticut, Nadia graduated from Columbia University, and earned an MA degree in Dance Therapy from Hunter College in New York. She and Enrico met in New York City and lived in the backwoods of upstate New York for eight years, before moving to California.

Complementing her background in dance therapy, Nadia has received certification in several somatic psychology disciplines, including Somatic Experiencing® (trauma therapy), biodynamic craniosacral therapy, and pre- and perinatal psychology. She is currently completing a PhD in clinical psychology at the Santa Barbara Graduate Institute. *The Blue Heron Ranch Cookbook* began as a labor of love and a form of relaxation from the intensity of her studies.

About the Illustrator

Marica Natali Thompson's passion for drawing began when she was a child growing up at Blue Heron Ranch. She is now writing and illustrating her own children's books, as well as collaborating with her mother Nadia on the sequel to *The Blue Heron Ranch Cookbook*. Marica lives in the mountains outside of Ojai with her husband Justin, and their three children, Samwise, Azalie, and Paolo.

Published by
North Atlantic Books
P.O. Box 12327
Berkeley, California 94712

and

Matilija Books
P.O. Box 1318
Ojai, California 93024

Cover art by Marica Natali Thompson
Cover and book design by Maxine Ressler
Production by Brad Greene
Printed in the United States of America

The Blue Heron Ranch Cookbook: Recipes and Stories from a Zen Retreat Center is sponsored by the Society for the Study of Native Arts and Sciences, a nonprofit educational corporation whose goals are to develop an educational and cross-cultural perspective linking various scientific, social, and artistic fields; to nurture a holistic view of arts, sciences, humanities, and healing; and to publish and distribute literature on the relationship of mind, body, and nature.

North Atlantic Books' publications are available through most bookstores. For further information, call 800-733-3000 or visit our website at www.northatlantic books.com

Library of Congress Cataloging-in-Publication Data

Natali, Nadia.
The Blue Heron Ranch cookbook : recipes and stories from a Zen retreat center / Nadia Natali ; illustrated by Marica Natali Thompson.
p. cm.
Summary: "Presents recipes from the Blue Heron Ranch Zen retreat center in California, with vignettes of how the Natali family brought the center into being"--Provided by publisher.
Includes bibliographical references and index.
ISBN 978-1-55643-717-5 (alk. paper)
1. Cookery, International. 2. Cookery, Asian. 3. Blue Heron Ranch (Retreat) I. Title.
TX725.A1N27 2008
641.9--dc22

2008008045

1 2 3 4 5 6 7 8 9 UNITED 14 13 12 11 10 09 08